Gentle
Discipline

Gentle Discipline

50 Effective Techniques for Teaching Your Children Good Behavior

By Dawn Lighter, M.A.

Meadowbrook Press
Distributed by Simon & Schuster
New York

Library of Congress Cataloging-in-Publication Data

Lighter, Dawn.
    Gentle discipline : 50 effective techniques for teaching your
children good behavior / by Dawn Lighter.
        p.   cm.
    Includes bibliographical references (p.   -   ).
    ISBN 0-88166-233-X
    1. Child rearing. 2. Discipline of children. 3. Parenting.
4. Parent and child. I. Title.
HQ769.L513   1995
649'.64—dc20   95-15373
                                                                CIP

Simon & Schuster Ordering # 0-671-52701-0

Published by Meadowbrook Press, 5451 Smetana Drive, Minnetonka,
MN 55343

BOOK TRADE DISTRIBUTION by Simon & Schuster,
a division of Simon and Schuster, Inc.,
1230 Avenue of the Americas, New York, NY 10020

Editor: Dale Howard
Production Manager: Amy Unger
Desktop Publishing Manager: Patrick Gross
Electronic Prepress Manager: Erik Broberg
Text Design: Amy Unger
Cover Photo: Telegraph Colour Library / FPG International Corp.

99 98 97   10 9 8 7 6 5 4 3

Printed in the United States of America

To my parents,
who gave me their shoulders to stand on

FOREWORD

WE HAVE A POPULAR SAYING IN OUR COUNTRY: "Spare the rod, spoil the child." It comes from the Bible, where the verse actually reads, "He who spares the rod hates his son, but he who loves him is diligent to discipline him" (Prov. 13:24). In biblical times, the rod was often used by shepherds to herd sheep. The main purpose of the rod was to guide the sheep and protect them from dangerous situations, not to hit them. This fact is supported by another verse that reads, "Thy rod and thy staff, they comfort me" (Psalm 23).

In this book, as in the Bible, good parenting is based on showing children love and respect, guiding them, teaching them, and protecting them from harm.

CONTENTS

THE 50 WAYS

People are doing what they have learned,
and it is the best they know.

—Virginia Satir

INTRODUCTION

SO YOU WANT TO BE A BETTER PARENT. MAYBE I CAN HELP. Just by opening this little book, you have shown that you care about your child; you have made a commitment. I am sure you are already a good parent. Perhaps I can give you some ideas to make your life a little easier, so you can do your job even better and make your home a happier place.

A few years ago, as part of my training to become a Marriage, Family, and Child Counselor, I worked at a counseling center in Escondido, California. Under the supervision of a licensed psychologist, I counseled many troubled children. I also met many dedicated, but exhausted, parents. These parents inspired me to write this book. They had tried everything they knew, but unfortunately their children continued to lie and steal, get into trouble at school, fight in the streets, or run away from home. It was very sad.

These parents clearly loved their children and wanted to help them but were feeling frustrated, embarrassed, and defeated. The children of these families varied in age. They lived in different neighborhoods and attended different schools. They represented a variety of races and religions, but these families were similar in one very important way: *the discipline at home was ineffective.*

Now, maybe you are one of the lucky ones. Maybe you are not having any big trouble with your child at home or at school. Maybe you won't have to suffer as other parents have. Whatever your present situation, I think parents with troubled children send a clear message that effective discipline is essential to the success and well-being of every child. Good discipline, I believe, is one of the keys to a happy home.

Discipline is a word often misunderstood. I feel the following two facts about discipline are important when working with children.

Good Discipline Is Not Punishment, It Is Instruction

PUNISHMENT BY ITSELF CAN MAKE A CHILD FEEL confused, angry, and rebellious, but effective discipline teaches appropriate behavior while eliminating inappropriate behavior. (Behavior will be described throughout this book as good/appropriate or bad/inappropriate.) Good discipline will help your child grow up feeling confident, responsible, and aware of his or her praiseworthy actions. Your child will need these tools to succeed.

Discipline Is Not Perfect

NO AMOUNT OF DISCIPLINE WILL GIVE YOU TOTAL CONTROL over your child. You have a very difficult job. Your child is growing up quickly. As a parent, you want to make sure that your child understands how the world works before he or she gets out there. Good discipline will help you develop a healthy parent-child relationship so that you can teach your child what he or she needs to know.

How well discipline works in your home depends on many things, including your child's age, your child's special needs, and the situation. Therefore, I encourage you to start developing a large "bag of tricks." A bag of tricks contains all the discipline ideas you have accumulated over the years. Some parents are fortunate to have bigger "bags" than others. You take what you need, and through trial and error, you discover what works and what doesn't. The important thing is that you don't give up.

As a student of human behavior, I developed a very large bag of tricks, numerous nonviolent ways to discipline children. I call the nonviolent ways the "higher" forms of discipline because, I believe, they reflect our evolution as thinking human beings. The fact that parents hit or spank their children (and most parents do), suggests to me that they are doing the best they can, but that they could probably use a few more tricks in their bag. It also suggests to me that they don't understand the negative effects of hitting as a form of discipline.

Following are four common reasons why people are opposed to hitting as a form of discipline for children.

Hitting Teaches Violence

AN EXAMPLE WILL ILLUSTRATE THIS POINT. I once worked with A very nice family who seemed typical in every way. The parents were young, intelligent, and middle-class. They had two sons, ages eleven and fourteen. Mom and dad were very upset because "Tommy," the eleven year old, was getting into fights regularly at school, a problem he had experienced since the third grade. Tommy's teacher complained that he picked on other classmates, especially children who were younger or disabled. Mom believed that the teacher was responsible for Tommy's aggressive behavior and considered moving him to another classroom or possibly another school. But, after meeting with the entire family, I learned the inevitable truth—Tommy was getting hit a lot at home, both by his parents and his older brother. I believe that they all had the best intentions and were only trying to discipline Tommy for his inappropriate behavior. However, I suggested to mom and dad that, as a first step in treatment, they take total responsibility for their son's discipline. (Tommy's older brother would have to save his parenting skills for the future.)

I also advised them to completely eliminate hitting as a form of discipline in their home.

Hopefully, from this example, you can understand how violence is learned in a family. Tommy learned *in his home* that hitting is a way to solve problems and deal with stressful situations. He learned that using extreme force against another person to get your point across is okay. In other words, "might is right." Tommy's parents used hitting as a way to demonstrate their dominance over him, and Tommy used hitting as a way to establish his dominance on the playground.

Hitting Can Be Dangerous to a Child, Both Physically and Psychologically

CORPORAL PUNISHMENT, IN CHILD REARING, IS DEFINED as the infliction of pain upon a child's body because of a mistake or act of disobedience. It does not include the temporary restraint of a child (*see* the Holding Technique, Way 33) or the removal of a weapon, such as a rock, from a child set on destruction (Maurer, *Corporal Punishment Handbook*, p. 1). Corporal punishment is typically carried out by means of a belt, wooden paddle, or human hand, but methods vary widely. Corporal punishment amounts to a big person hitting a little person, and the risk of physical injury is enormous. Did you know, for example, that hitting a child in the face or head area can cause permanent damage to the child's eyes, ears, and brain? (Taylor and Maurer, *Think Twice*).

Children who are hit can develop psychological problems, such as extreme anger and aggressive behavior. They often suffer from low self-esteem as well. Simply put, to a child, being hit means that he or she is a bad person, not that his or her behavior is bad or inappropriate.

Hitting Is Ineffective

STUDIES SHOW THAT HITTING IS AN INEFFECTIVE WAY to discipline a child (McCormick, "Attitudes of Primary Care Physicians Toward Corporal Punishment" p. 3161). It is thought to be more effective in letting out a parent's built-up tension than as a way of controlling a child. In the short run, hitting can make a child behave better, but in the long run, it can create more problems for both parent and child. Parents, for example, can suffer from feelings of guilt and remorse. And children can miss out on the opportunity to learn important coping skills from their parents—skills they will need for the future, such as how to solve problems through the use of reason, and how to express anger in healthy, nonviolent ways.

Hitting Can Get You in Trouble with the Law

CHILD ABUSE REPORTING LAWS ARE CURRENTLY IN EFFECT nationwide. Although physical abuse has numerous definitions, it is generally described as *any act by an adult that results in the nonaccidental physical injury of a child.* Unfortunately, this type of injury can occur when an angry or frustrated parent strikes a child. Punishment for child abuse varies from state to state, but the removal of children from their homes is common practice in cases of abuse.

How you choose to discipline your child is a very important matter. The decisions you make as a parent will depend on the number of options you have and the amount of information you have gathered. My purpose then, in writing this book, is to provide you with a feast of new parenting ideas, options, and information, so that you can make the best decisions possible for you and your child.

In this book, you will find fifty ways to build a healthy, happy relationship with your child. For your convenience, I have divided them

INTRODUCTION

into five key parts. Part One offers simple and effective ways to avoid conflict with your child. Part Two focuses on specific ways to improve communication between you and your child. This includes both verbal and nonverbal forms of communication. Part Three details ways to control your child's behavior by shaping and manipulating your child's environment. Part Four discusses the importance of giving your child consequences. I describe numerous ways to encourage appropriate behavior and discourage inappropriate behavior in your child. Finally, Part Five addresses your needs as a parent. I will teach you how to lower stress in your life and develop support systems. I will recommend a variety of ways to stay in shape, both physically and psychologically, so that you can feel your best and function better as a parent.

Take your time reading the 50 Ways. I recommend that you read one or two Ways and then put the book down. Give yourself a full day to digest what you have read and to think about how it could work for you and your family. I wish you great success as you travel down the road to a healthier and happier relationship with your child.

D. L.

LEARNING FROM OUR PARENTS

THERE IS NO SUCH THING AS A PERFECT CHILDHOOD. It is a stressful time for many reasons. When you remember your childhood, what do you recall? You can probably remember certain events that had a lasting effect on you. Perhaps your parents divorced when you were young, and you found yourself moving with one parent to a strange new home in an unfamiliar neighborhood. You may remember a special birthday or holiday celebration. Are your memories mostly happy, or are they filled with a sense of sadness, discomfort, or regret? What type of parents did you have growing up? Parenting styles can be very different, but they are sometimes divided into three general types: Authoritarian, Permissive, and Authoritative.

If your parents were *authoritarian*, they were very strict with you and may have seemed powerful and threatening in some ways. You were forced to accept their values and follow their way of doing things at all times. Although they loved you, they probably did not show you a lot of physical affection, and your behavior was more often punished than rewarded. Your authoritarian parents set up strict house rules that were difficult to follow, especially as you got older and your needs changed. You probably felt that your authoritarian parents had trouble understanding you and accepting you. They were generally intolerant of thoughts and ideas different from their own. You probably felt that they were constantly trying to control you, correct you, and mold you in the hope that one day you would live up to their idea of the perfect child— live up to their expectations. Of course, you couldn't then, and you should stop trying now. A person can never be happy trying to live up to the expectations of others.

If your parents were *permissive*, you grew up in a house with love, but one that was not very well organized or maintained. Few demands and restrictions were placed on you. You were neither punished nor rewarded on a regular basis. It was probably a little difficult and frustrating to live in a permissive household. Your parents did not always act responsibly toward you. They may have neglected to teach you important things or give you the skills that you needed to be independent. Unfortunately, you had to learn these skills the hard way, without their guidance and support.

If you grew up with *authoritative* parents, you had a definite advantage. Your parents were teachers in many ways. They taught you how to act in a mature and responsible way, and they rewarded you when you did. Your authoritative parents were very loving and affectionate toward you. You felt as though they really listened to you, and they encouraged you to think for yourself. The house rules were reasonable and based on your age and your particular needs. The rules changed over time to allow you more freedom and responsibility. There were consequences when you broke the rules, but your behavior was more often rewarded than punished. You grew up with a sense of your uniqueness as a person and with the skills to be independent.

According to Dr. Charles Whitfield, author of *Healing the Child Within*, roughly 80 to 95 percent of adults grow up in families where they do not receive the amount of love, guidance, and nurturing necessary "to form consistently healthy relationships, and to feel good about themselves and about what they do" (p. 2).

While it is true that many families are troubled, my intention is not to upset you, but rather to offer you hope and comfort: comfort, for example, in knowing that most of us come from less-than-perfect families, and hope, because no matter what type of family you grew up in— whether it was very troubled, not troubled at all, or somewhere in between—you can evolve. You have the ability to grow and develop, both as a person and as a parent.

I believe you must take three steps to experience change and growth in your life. The first step is *awareness.* If the foundation for adulthood is laid in childhood, then you should understand (if you don't already) something about the family from which you came. It was there, in your family of origin, that you first learned how to communicate and interact with others, to express anger, to give and receive love, and, of course, to be a parent.

As you take this first step, you may become aware of any issues (problems or conflicts) that stem from your childhood; for example, issues of trust, low self-esteem, or selfless behavior that denies your personal needs. I urge you to resolve any issues in your life as soon as possible, not only because they can cause you tremendous emotional pain, but because they can prevent you from growing and developing as a person (*see* Way 49, Individual Therapy for You).

The second step in the growth process is to *learn new skills.* Skill building is essential to success in every aspect of your life. It involves empowering yourself with new information to help you cope with the challenges of a fast-changing world. As a parent, for example, you should educate yourself on normal child development to learn what is appropriate and inappropriate behavior for your child (*see* Suggested Readings and Referral Information, page 101). You will also need a wide assortment of practical skills—not only discipline skills, but also skills for improving communication with your child and for controlling your anger. Remember that to give up old habits and ineffective ways of interacting, you must have new methods of interacting to replace them. Give yourself the skills to improve your life and your relationships.

The final step is to *get support.* Change and growth as a parent involves risk taking, and this can be scary, especially if you grew up with parents who were poor role models. When you learn new ways of doing things and try those new techniques, you may feel awkward and uncomfortable. This discomfort may lead you to retreat to familiar, and less-effective, ways of parenting. For this reason, it is important to get the support you need (*see* Way 50, Join Parents Anonymous).

As a parent, you are only one part of the family. But you are an important part. A change in you equals a change in them. Growth for you means growth for them. Your parents did the best job they could with you. Now it's your turn. So, let's begin.

Please Note: The 50 Ways are designed for children of various ages and stages of development. At the end of each Way, you will find a recommendation for a specific age group. Ages are grouped as follows:

Under 2	=	Infants, children under 2 years of age
2–5	=	Preschool-age, children about 2 to 5 years old
6–12	=	School-age, children 6 to 12 years old
Teenagers	=	Teenage children 13 to 19 years old

These recommendations should serve only as a general guideline for you and your child. If you know or suspect that your child has a physical or mental disability, please consult your family doctor before using any of the discipline methods described in this book. **Above all, never risk your child's health or safety.**

THE
50 WAYS
PART ONE
Ten Ways to Avoid
Conflict with Your Child

1. Ignore the Inappropriate Behavior

A GREAT, TRUE STORY TELLS ABOUT A LITTLE GIRL who would go to school every day and bang her head against a wall. Well, naturally, everyone in her classroom, including her teacher, became frantic at this sight. They all ran to her rescue and tried to comfort her in any way they could. Finally, after several days, a psychologist got involved in the little girl's sad case. Without the child knowing, he advised her teacher and classmates to ignore her each time she banged her head. The next day, the little girl arrived at school and banged her head in the usual way, but the class ignored her. The day after, she was ignored again. As the days passed, the little girl gradually began to bang her head less and less. Finally, one day, she stopped the inappropriate behavior completely.

I admit, the story of the little girl is an extreme example, but I think it demonstrates an important point: sometimes parents encourage children to misbehave by giving them attention when they do. Attention can be positive (such as praise) or negative (such as criticism), but in the case of inappropriate behavior, sometimes no attention is the best remedy. If you believe that your attention is contributing to your child's inappropriate behavior, try withholding it. The "ignoring technique" can be very effective with children, especially when parents do it right. Here are some things to keep in mind:

- **No attention means absolutely no attention.** Don't respond to your child in any way—don't yell at, look at, or talk to your child. (While being fully aware of your child, use this time to do other activities.)

- Ignore your child completely for the entire time he or she is demonstrating the inappropriate behavior. This could last five minutes or twenty-five minutes, so be prepared.

- Be sure that other adults or family members in the room cooperate with you and also ignore the child.

- Finally, be ready to praise your child the moment he or she stops the inappropriate behavior. You might say, for example, "I'm so glad you stopped throwing that temper tantrum. I don't like temper tantrums because the screaming hurts my ears. It's easier to be around you now that you aren't screaming." The "ignoring technique" asks you, above all, to be patient, and to remember that you are *not* ignoring the child, you are ignoring the behavior.

Children under 2/2–5/6–12/Teenagers

2. Walk Away

I ONCE MET A YOUNG, HOMELESS MOTHER who had a very well-behaved five-year-old daughter sitting beside her. I asked the mother what her secret was for getting the child to behave. She told me that whenever her daughter acts out or throws a tantrum, she simply walks away, sits down somewhere, and smokes a cigarette. From a distance she can watch her child and protect her from any harm, if necessary. By walking away, this mother avoids giving in to her child's demands; she stays in control. Children of all ages sometimes push their parents to the breaking point—the point where the parents lose control. Older children can

surprise their parents with a houseful of damage when they decide to disobey rules such as "No playing ball in the living room" or "No parties in the house without adult supervision." If you find yourself losing control with your child and you need a short break, don't hesitate to take one (*see* Way 42, Learn to Relax). Give yourself and your child an opportunity to calm down. Smoking is optional but not recommended.
Children under 2/2-5/6-12/Teenagers

3. Use Distraction

ONE WAY TO AVOID A PROBLEM SITUATION is to use distraction. Children, especially infants and very young children, are easily distracted; they have short attention spans and are constantly stimulated by things in their environment. If you see your child headed in a bad direction, try to get his or her attention. If your child is very young, you might say things like, "Look over there! What do you see? It's a mirror! Can you make a funny face?" You can also redirect your child over to you with words like, "Come and sit on my lap. I want to read you a story."

Distraction can be used with older children as well. For example, you can interrupt a round of sibling rivalry by suggesting a video game or movie. Sometimes children will drop whatever they are doing to be a part of adult activities. You might say to your child, "Come and help me in the kitchen (or garage, or backyard). You can be my assistant."

If your words are friendly, enthusiastic, and playful, your child is likely to stop what he or she is doing and follow your directions.
Children under 2/2-5/6-12/Teenagers

4. Use Substitution

IF A CHILD IS DOING SOMETHING INAPPROPRIATE, give the child something appropriate to do. Children need to be taught *how* and *when* and *where* to be appropriate. It is not enough for them to know their behavior is unacceptable. They should be given a substitute or alternative behavior, whenever possible. Here are some examples:

- If a child is using a crayon on a sofa, substitute with a coloring book.

- If a child is getting into mother's makeup and making a mess, substitute with children's makeup that rinses off easily.

- If a child is throwing rocks into the street, substitute with a baseball and play a game of catch.

If your child is playing with something that is breakable or off limits, try to find a substitute game or toy that he or she can enjoy. Children are constantly looking for outlets for their creativity and physical energy.

Learning to find quick and inexpensive substitutes for your child's inappropriate behavior is your insurance against many future problems.

Children under 2/2-5/6-12/Teenagers

5. Find the Positive

NO ONE LIKES TO BE CRITICIZED. Criticism hurts! Children who are criticized are likely to feel angry and defensive. Consequently, they will be less likely to cooperate. But, as you know, criticizing a child's inappropriate behavior is sometimes necessary. So how can you criticize your child without creating a conflict? Gently, of course. We are all familiar with the expression "A spoonful of sugar makes the medicine go down." If you sweeten the criticism, the child may respond to it, and to you, better. I recommend that parents soften harsh words with a small dose of praise. Here are some examples:

- **Parent:** "I think you have a beautiful voice, but singing is not allowed at the dinner table."

- **Parent:** "You are a great soccer player, but kicking belongs on the soccer field—not in the classroom."

- **Parent:** "Thank you for telling me the truth, but next time I want you to ask my permission before you go to your friend's house."

I worked with a teenage girl, "Anne," who skipped school one day to comfort a friend who was going through a family crisis and wanted to run away from home. Anne's mother was furious with her. I agreed that skipping school is bad but pointed out that Anne's behavior also proved she is a caring and supportive friend. Finding the negative in a child's inappropriate behavior is easy. The next time your child does something you don't like, I challenge you to find the positive.

Children under 2/2-5/6-12/Teenagers

6. Offer Choices

HAVE YOU EVER WONDERED WHY A CHILD is sometimes so willing to reject a parent's idea or direction? The answer is simple: it is the child's natural way of asserting his or her independence. One way to avoid such a conflict with your child is to offer choices. You can offer choices to your child throughout the day in a variety of situations. Here are some examples:

- Food: "Do you want eggs or cereal for breakfast?"
   "Would you like carrots or corn with your dinner?"

- Clothes: "Would you like to wear your blue or yellow shirt to school?"
   "Do you want to dress yourself or shall I help you?"

- Chores: "Are you going to do your chores before or after dinner?"
   "Would you rather take out the garbage or do the dishes?"

Choices are important because they encourage children to think for themselves. Children gain a healthy sense of power and self-esteem by making decisions on their own. Parents, meanwhile, are able to support their child's need for independence and still maintain some control over the child's behavior.

Children under 2/2-5/6-12/Teenagers

7. Use Humor

SOMETHING HAPPENED TO US ON THE ROCKY ROAD TO ADULTHOOD. We started taking life very seriously—too seriously, perhaps. Children, for example, laugh an outrageous 400 times a day, while we grown-ups laugh about fifteen times a day (Corridan and Hoch, "Fun Facts," p. 80). Let's face it, we could use more humor in our adult lives and especially in our relationships with children. Humor is a wonderful way for us to relieve tension, both physically and mentally, and to cope with difficult situations.

I remember an experience I once had while working at a shelter for homeless and battered women. I was listening to a woman describe her ongoing battle to free herself from her abusive husband, when suddenly we were interrupted by a small child, the woman's daughter, who proceeded to present her case (to go swimming, I think) in a whining, demanding voice. This mother did not wait long to respond, but rather than give her daughter the usual command, "Stop whining!", she reacted playfully. Using an exaggerated style, she performed a humorous imitation of her daughter—complete with whining voice, hand gestures, and facial expressions. "Mom!" the mother wailed, "I want to go swimming, Mom! Hurry, Mom, take me now!" Within seconds, the little girl saw the humor in the situation. She squealed with delight at the sight of her mother acting like a child. Mother and daughter laughed and relaxed together. And the next time the little girl spoke to her mother, I noticed she wasn't whining.

Doing a lighthearted exaggeration is one way to bring humor to a tense situation. Here are some other ideas: try using fantasy and make-believe with young children. Bring inanimate objects to life (your ventriloquist skills will come in handy here). Use books, cups, shoes, socks, whatever you need to get your point across. A child who refuses to put his or her toys away may reconsider when a toy tearfully cries out, "It's late and I'm very tired. I want to go home. Will you help me?" Or if your child does not want to brush his or her teeth, perhaps you could engage your child in a conversation with the toothbrush.

Hint: If you find at some point that your trick is no longer giving you the results you need, try a variation of a similar theme. For example, you could have a contest with your child to see who can brush their teeth the longest.

Another idea is simply to say something ridiculous. For example, to motivate your child to clean, you might say, "This room smells so bad, I think there are dinosaur bones buried here!" Or, "If we don't clean up soon, the U.S. Department of Dust Busters is going to quarantine this house!" You can also leave funny notes for your child to find: to a teenager, "Remember to be home by 10:00 P.M. Signed, the Pajama Search Party."

Try being silly and spontaneous. Make a funny face or speak in a strange voice. Sing loudly or off key. You can also change the words to a popular song to suit your needs. For example, to the Barney tune, "I Love You," you could sing:

> **Time for school,**
> **Don't be late;**
> **You have got an important date.**
> **The teacher's waiting and she wants you there,**
> **So, brush your teeth and comb your hair.**

You can do something completely unexpected when the pressure starts to build. Let your child eat breakfast food for dinner or wear school clothes to bed or stay up past bedtime. Don't be afraid to break a minor rule once in a while to avoid a conflict. Your child will still know you are the boss.

A word of caution: when using humor in your home, try to be sensitive to your child. Avoid cruel or sarcastic remarks. If your child is insecure about certain things, such as braces or pimples or big ears, don't make jokes about them.

Humor in parenting involves exaggeration and make-believe. It is silly and spontaneous, ridiculous and unexpected. It is also inexpensive and easy to find. Best of all, it teaches us that we don't have to do things perfectly all the time (because tying our shoelaces wrong can be funny). Humor gives us permission to relax and lose our inhibitions for a moment or two, and be a kid again.

Children under 2/2-5/6-12/Teenagers

8. Model Appropriate Behavior

CHILDREN OFTEN BEHAVE IN WAYS WE FIND INAPPROPRIATE; sometimes they need an adult to stop and show them a better way. As a parent, you are the person your child will imitate more than anyone else. And because of this, modeling is the best and easiest way to teach your child. Modeling is simply learning by observation. In other words, your child will learn what is appropriate behavior by watching and imitating you.

You can model an unlimited number of appropriate behaviors for your child. Here are some examples:

- Infant:

  Making good eye contact.

  Showing empathy.

  Expressing love with affection.

- Preschool-age:

  Sitting patiently.

  Sharing things with others.

  Resolving conflict without fighting.

- School Age:

  Answering the telephone properly.

  Caring for pets in a humane and responsible way.

  Spending money wisely.

- Teenagers:

  Talking without yelling.

  Listening without interrupting.

  Saying "No" to drugs and alcohol.

By modeling appropriate behaviors for your child now, you will avoid many conflicts in the future. You can also feel proud knowing that your child has learned something from you—something good.

Children under 2/2-5/6-12/Teenagers

9. Choose Your Battles

NO PARENT WANTS TO TURN A HOME INTO A BATTLEFIELD, and yet, it can sometimes happen. One of my clients, a teenage boy, told me his mother complained a lot about his behavior. She complained about his eating habits, his sleeping habits, his hair, his clothes, his bedroom, his friends, his school performance, and the way he spent his days. His response to his mother was to "tune her out." When I spoke to the mother, it became clear that what she really wanted was for the boy to get a part-time job. Unfortunately, her request for him to get a job was lost in a sea of other requests. To the boy, mom's disapproving words began to sound like static. He became so angry at her for making so many requests of him that, as a result, he fought her every step of the way.

If you find that your child has numerous inappropriate behaviors you would like to change, it is time to stop and take inventory. Ask yourself which behaviors are the most important and must be dealt with immediately. Throw out the ones that seem petty by comparison.

Set priorities, and then take action.

Children 2-5/6-12/Teenagers

10. Set Age-Appropriate Limits

FROM ABOUT THE AGE OF FIVE MONTHS, if all goes well, children will begin their struggle for independence. Their goal is to become complete and separate human beings, capable of doing and thinking for themselves. By setting age-appropriate limits for your child, you are recognizing his or her goal of independence. Base your rules and limits on your child's age, ability, particular needs, and level of responsibility, so that he or she can safely reach this goal.

Some parents make the mistake of treating their children exactly the same, regardless of their age differences or individual needs. I once had a counseling client, a sixteen-year-old girl, who wanted a simple daytime lock on her bedroom door—a very normal request from a teenager. The girl's father said "No" because he felt that if he gave her a lock, he would have to give one to all his children (ages five and up), and he did not want to live in a "prison."

Unfortunately, the father in this case did not understand that, while his five year old was not responsible enough to maintain a locked bedroom door, his teenage daughter certainly was, and with an inexpensive lock, he could satisfy her need for privacy.

So build your home on solid ground, but make sure that your rules are flexible. This does not mean you should let your child break your rules, but you must be ready to set new rules and limits as your child gets older and his or her needs change.

New rules, in general, should offer a child a little more responsibility and freedom—not only the freedom to go more places and do more things, but the freedom to make more decisions independently. By slowly and carefully expanding your limits, you will meet your child's need for greater independence. This way, your child will not have to rebel to get the freedom he or she deserves.

To understand your child better at every age, see Suggested Readings and Referral Information, page 101. I have also provided the following general guideline for normal child behavior.

Children Under 2 Years

INFANTS DISCOVER THE WORLD THROUGH THEIR SENSES—taste, touch, smell, sight, and sound. A twelve month old, for example, may drop a cup from a highchair in order to understand object permanence (the idea that objects continue to exist even after they are out of sight). Infants communicate their feelings by cooing, babbling, and crying. And despite the noise and mess they sometimes make, this is not the time to establish numerous rules; infants learn rules slowly (one at a time is best), beginning around fifteen months. Above all, infants need to be cared for in a consistent and predictable way. They need to feel safe, loved, and secure.

Children 2–5 Years

PRESCHOOLERS ARE ADVENTUROUS PEOPLE. They have the energy, curiosity, and boldness to take on new activities. Parents should encourage independent behavior by giving preschoolers plenty of room to explore. But they must also set limits to keep the children safe. Preschoolers have difficulty distinguishing fantasy from reality—nightmares and daydreams are real; so are imaginary friends. Play becomes a central part of their life. They sometimes act out roles such as "doctor and patient" or "mommy and child" as a way to express their wishes and fears. Through play, they also develop such social skills as reciprocity. A certain amount of aggression is normal in preschoolers (children will, for example, fight over a toy), so parents need to teach them, at this early age, how to resolve conflicts in a nonaggressive manner. Preschool is the time when children learn how to get along with others, first in a play environment, then in the real world.

Children 6-12 Years

SCHOOL-AGED CHILDREN ARE INDUSTRIOUS PEOPLE. They work hard to develop their skills, both in and out of the classroom. Whether they are riding a bicycle, doing arithmetic, or building a fort, they need to feel competent at what they do. Compared to preschoolers, school-aged children are more responsible and less dependent on their parents; they can make more decisions on their own. Parents can help school-aged children by giving them support and encouragement in their school work. They can also provide opportunities for their children to succeed through various clubs (computer, scouting, 4-H) or athletic organizations, such as Little League Baseball. Parents must have realistic expectations. For example, expect your child to *do* his or her best, rather than to *be* the best. Through their accomplishments, school-aged children develop a healthy self-esteem. They gain the strength and the confidence to strive for goals in the future.

Teenagers 13-19 Years

TEENAGERS HAVE THE DIFFICULT TASK of developing their own, separate identities. They have to figure out *who* they are, *where* they want to go, and *how* they are going to get there. To do this, they need many things, including the support of their parents and friends. Friends provide a support group in which teenagers can learn social skills, share problems, test their ideas, and strengthen their identity. Parents provide teenagers with clear communication skills (especially, good listening), love and affection, and a strong set of family values. For example, parents should express their disapproval of stealing, lying, alcohol, and drug use. Teenagers need a great amount of freedom in order to test the waters of adulthood, but they also need discipline. Parents should set reasonable limits for their teenagers with regard to homework and curfew. Like children of all ages, teenagers need love and limits (though not as many), with the help of which they will grow up to be self-confident, responsible, and independent human beings.

THE
50 WAYS
PART TWO
Ten Ways to Improve Communication

11. Give Clear and Specific Commands

PARENTS OFTEN GIVE THEIR CHILDREN DIRECTIONS such as, "Be good," "Behave yourself," "Stay out of trouble," or "Don't make me mad." Unfortunately, these commands are vague, abstract, and often confuse children. Make your commands very clear and specific. Here are some examples:

- Infants:
  "No!"
  "No biting!"

- Preschoolers:
  "Stop running in the house."
  "Eat your cereal."

- School-age:
  "Come inside now."
  "Sit on the chair and be quiet."

- Teenagers:
  "Turn your stereo volume down."
  "Don't use swear words in the house."

Try to make sentences short and keep your vocabulary simple—explain any words your child does not know. If your child is able to talk in complete sentences (beginning around age three), you can ask him or her to repeat the command back to you. This way the child is more likely to understand the command and remember it.

Hint: If your child seems unable or unwilling to follow your command, wait sixty seconds, then try using Distraction (Way 3) with children under 2, Time Out (Way 34) for children 2 through 12, and Taking Away a Privilege (Way 37) for teenagers.

Children, at every age, spend a lot of their time trying to please adults. By giving your child specific instructions, you will help him or her avoid inappropriate behavior and win your approval.

Children under 2/2-5/6-12/Teenagers

12. Use Body Language Effectively

YOUR BODY LANGUAGE IS AN IMPORTANT PART of the message you give your child. If you want to make a strong statement or give a command, be sure that your body is consistent with your words. Sometimes, parents call out commands to their children from a relaxed position, for example, from a sofa as they watch TV or read a newspaper. They might say something like, "Stop throwing the ball in the house!" or "Don't hit your sister!" Their words are strong, but their body language is weak and indifferent. Any time your words and your body language don't match, it is called a *mixed message*. A mixed message is indirect and confusing, which means that your child is less likely to stop the inappropriate behavior.

So what are some ways you can make a strong statement with your body? First, try to talk to your child directly; look into his or her eyes when you speak. Stand straight. Put your hands at your waist or point a finger. Try snapping your fingers or clapping your hands once or twice to get your child's full attention. Just keep your body language consistent with your words, so that your commands to your child come through loud and clear.

Children under 2/2-5/6-12/Teenagers

13. Say "No!" and Mean It

HOW DO YOU SAY "NO" TO YOUR CHILD? Children will generally respond to the tone of your voice. A "No!" command should be spoken in a firm, clear way. It is good to raise your voice above your normal speaking tone, but it is not necessary to scream or yell (except in cases of emergency).

How do you use the word "No"? Parents often give their children a mixed or confusing message: sometimes "No" means "Maybe," or it could mean "Ask me again later." The mother of a teenaged girl once told me that she will change a "No" to a "Yes" when "my daughter wears me out." If you feel that your child is trying to wear you out or manipulate you into changing your mind, simply stop talking. *Stay calm.* Let your child vent his or her frustration on you. Once you have said "No" to your child and given your reason, you do not have to answer more questions. (I recommend a short, simple reason, one that your child can understand.) You do not have to defend your position to your child—you are not the defendant in a trial, you are the judge. *This is an important point*, so I would like you to take a moment to visualize yourself in the role of a courtroom judge. Now imagine yourself saying "No" to your child. As a judge-parent, you would remain calm and rational as you stated your final decision. Your words would be like gold; you would choose them very carefully and use them sparingly.

Never forget that you are the judge in your family, and your words give you your power.

And the next time you feel your child trying to put you into the defendant's chair, a good response to him or her would be, "I gave you my answer. My answer is 'No.'" You can then either ignore your child's behavior or repeat those simple words over and over in a calm, clear way until your child is able to accept them.

Hint: If your child refuses to follow your "No!" command, try calling Time Out (Way 34). If you are not in a position to do Time Out with your child (for example, if you are sitting in a doctor's office), then take a half hour off your child's bedtime.

Children under 2/2-5/6-12/Teenagers

14. Talk to Your Child Calmly

THIS APPROACH REMINDS ME OF THAT OLD SAYING about the bees: "You can get more honey from a bee with sugar than with vinegar." The idea here is that children can be as troublesome as bees at times, so parents must know how to use a little "sugar" to stop their child's inappropriate behavior. I recommend that parents talk to their child in a calm, nonthreatening way. This means that if you are feeling extremely angry about something your child did, then you must take some time to cool down (*see* Learn to Relax, Way 42).

In general, although responding to inappropriate behavior immediately is best, in this case, I advise you to make an exception. Your body should be relaxed and nonthreatening, consistent with your words.

Speak slowly and choose your words very carefully. If your words attack your child in any way, he or she is likely to feel bullied and hurt, angry, defensive, and even rebellious. On the other hand, if you talk in a calm, nonthreatening way, you will encourage your child to trust you, listen to you, and cooperate with you in the future.

So what are some nonthreatening ways in which you can talk to your child about his or her behavior? First, and perhaps most important, speak to your child as you would like to be spoken to. Don't yell (yelling is *always* harsh and threatening to children). Always avoid verbal put-downs or name-calling. Also, instead of beginning your sentences with "You," try using "I" statements when talking to your child about his or her inappropriate behavior. For example, instead of saying "You keep your room like a pig pen," or "You are a bad girl for hitting your brother," try beginning your sentences with "I": "I was really upset when I saw your room this morning. I think we should all try to keep our house clean. I want you to choose one day each week to clean your room," or "I am afraid you are going to hurt your brother. Please stop hitting him."

Notice that in the "I" statements, you tell your child how his or her behavior makes you feel. In cases like these, express to your child that you are unhappy with his or her behavior.

Talking is the most important part of the discipline process. By using words that show sensitivity, honesty, and respect, you are more likely to gain your child's cooperation, and you will leave the door open for good communication in your relationship.

Children under 2/2–5/6–12/Teenagers

15. Be a Good Listener

IF YOUR CHILD IS OLD ENOUGH TO TALK about his or her inappropriate behavior, stop and listen if you can. Try to understand what your child is feeling inside. This is sometimes hard to do. It means setting time aside so that you can give your child your full attention. Move down to your child's level and sit close together. Make good eye contact. Don't interrupt when your child is talking. Give your child the freedom to talk about his or her feelings. Whether you agree or disagree with the way your child feels, know that your child has a right to his or her feelings. *Feelings are okay.* It is only behavior—the way your child acts out certain feelings—that can be inappropriate. For example, for your child to be mad at his or her friend is okay, but to spit in the friend's face is not okay.

To be a good listener, you must have a variety of skills. I recommend that you read *How to Talk So Kids Will Listen and Listen So Kids Will Talk* by Adele Faber and Elaine Mazlish. I have also put together the following list of basic listening skills for parents:

- **Give direct, concerned attention.**

- **Maintain eye contact at your child's level, if possible.**

- **Find a way to show your child that you are listening to what he or she is saying.** For example, you can respond back with words like, "Oh," "I see," "No kidding," "Uh-huh," "Wow," and "Please go on."

- Validate your child's feelings by communicating understanding and concern. For example:
  Child (angrily): "A boy at school today took my ball!"
  Parent (validating): "That must have made you really mad!"

- Use reflective listening, repeating back what you hear your child saying. For example:
  Child: "I don't like my teacher because she embarrasses me in class."
  Parent (reflecting): "You feel as though your teacher sometimes embarrasses you."

By reflecting back your child's words, you will make your child feel listened to, understood, and affirmed. When used along with your other skills, reflective listening enables you to keep the conversation open, so that your child feels comfortable expressing more thoughts and feelings.

As you listen to your child, consider whether his or her inappropriate behavior is a sign of a bigger, more serious problem. Many behaviors seen among children, such as fighting in school, using drugs, or hurting animals, are only signs of a deeper problem. Children who constantly get into trouble or act out inappropriately are really suffering inside and need special attention. In cases like these, I suggest that parents get a professional opinion.

The more you listen to your child, the more information you will gather. In this way, you will learn the truth about your child's behavior so that you can deal with it effectively.

Children under 2/2-5/6-12/Teenagers

16. Try to Solve the Problem

SOMETIMES A CHILD'S INAPPROPRIATE BEHAVIOR results from a situation that is not working; there is a problem that must be solved. Because you are older and more experienced, it is likely that you can help. Here is a simple three-step process that can be used to solve many behavior problems.

Note: Before you begin, make sure that you are calm and thinking clearly. Never try to solve a serious problem in the heat of a fight or battle with your child.

Step 1: Define the problem.

Define the problem in clear and simple terms. Focus on one problem at a time. Here is an example:

Katie, age seven, sometimes forgets to do her household chores.

Step 2: Brainstorm.

Think of a number of possible solutions to the problem. If your child is old enough to participate, I suggest that you sit down together and brainstorm. It can help to write down your ideas on paper. Consider the advantages and disadvantages of each decision.

Step 3: Choose a solution.

Try to give your child as much control as possible in choosing a solution. He or she is more likely to cooperate this way. In the above example, the parent and child agreed on the following:

Each week, Katie will make a list of "Things to Do." This list will include her weekly chores and other important things to remember.

She will keep her list of "Things to Do" posted in her bathroom at home, on the kitchen refrigerator, and in her desk at school.

Often, scolding or punishing a child for his or her behavior is not enough; parents may also need to ask, "What is the problem?" and "How can I help?"

Children under 2/2–5/6–12/Teenagers

17. Know How to Use Threats

SOMETIMES PARENTS WANT TO AVOID giving their child a negative consequence, so they warn the child and threaten him or her with a future consequence. (Consequences are discussed in Part Four of The 50 Ways.) Yes, you *can* control your child's behavior with threats, but threats are effective only when used occasionally—not as a regular means of discipline. Threats should tell your child in a clear and specific way what the consequence will be in the future if he or she chooses not to cooperate. Avoid making threats with vague, uncertain consequences. The child may have trouble understanding or accepting them. You may tell a child, for example, that if he or she does not come straight home from school today, then he or she cannot go to the amusement park on Saturday.

Threats should only be given if the consequence is realistic and fair, and if you are willing to carry it out. I once heard a father threaten to put his little boy in an institution for his inappropriate behavior. Besides scaring his child unnecessarily, this father was relying on an empty threat; he had no intention of carrying out this extreme consequence.

Children will eventually learn whether their parents' threats are empty, and Mom and Dad will be back to square one, working harder than ever to control their child's behavior. So be smart—don't start (as the saying goes). Keep your threats clear and fair, and be ready to carry them out at all times.

Children 2-5/6-12/Teenagers

18. Write a Behavior Contract

HAVE YOU EVER NOTICED THAT REMEMBERING THINGS IS EASIER when you write them down? Behavior contracts are good for that reason. Your child is more likely to remember the rules you wish to enforce when they are documented on paper. Behavior contracts are commonly used by mental health professionals, parents, and teachers because they are effective and easy to use. Here is how a simple behavior contract works.

In Step 1, write down in very clear terms what you want your child to do or not do. (It is best to limit the contract to one behavior at a time.) For example:

John will go to bed each night at 8:30 P.M.

In Step 2, write down the way in which you will check your child's behavior. Ask yourself, "Who will be responsible for checking the behavior? How often will the behavior be checked?" For example:

Mom or Dad will go into John's room each night at approximately 8:30 P.M. to see if John is in bed, in his pajamas, with the lights off.

In Step 3, write down the negative consequence that your child will receive if he or she does not do the desired behavior.

If John is not in bed, in his pajamas, with the lights off at 8:30 P.M., he will not be allowed to play outside the following day. (On a school day, John will be required to come home directly after school).

In Step 4, offer your child a reward for appropriate behavior. (Rewards are discussed in Part Four of The 50 Ways.) Although you do not have to use rewards in a behavior contract, I strongly recommend that you do.

(Optional) If John obeys the terms of the contract, he can have a friend over to play one day each week.

Always choose a reward that is of high value to your child; this way, he or she will be more motivated to perform the desired behavior.

Then, decide when the contract will go into effect. Today? Next week? Write the effective date at the top of the contract. Go over all the terms of the contract with your child to make sure that your child understands the contract completely, then both of you sign it.

There are two additional things to remember: First, discuss the contract with any other caretakers in the house (husband, wife, grandmother), so that they understand the rules of the contract and will uphold them. Second, if you make any changes in the contract, be sure to inform your child, and both of you should sign the new or revised copy.

Behavior contracts are useful when dealing with problem behaviors because they enable you to think and plan a strategy for yourself and your child. Like preparing yourself for an earthquake, your contract will let you know ahead of time what to do when the bad event happens.

Children 6–12/Teenagers

19. Hold Family Meetings

ONE HOUR-LONG MEETING, ONE DAY A WEEK, and you can keep your family moving on a steady, even course. The family meeting is the time when you will check the pulse of each member and find out who is hurting, who needs help. This is your "quality time" as a family, when individual members can express their concerns and fears, when problem situations are uncovered and possible solutions are discussed. Encourage each child and adult to talk about his or her life, how it is going in general, and what, if anything, isn't working. Start your family meetings with some basic ground rules. I suggest the following:

- **The adults are responsible for leading the group and enforcing all rules.**

- **Each member of the family must attend except in unusual circumstances.**

- **Each member may express an opinion whether others agree or disagree with it.**

- **No yelling.**

- **No interrupting when someone else is talking.**

- **No put-downs or name-calling.**

- **No distractions (TV off, radio off).**

- Each member may offer possible solutions to the various problems that come up at the meeting (try to decide on solutions everyone can agree on).

- The adults are responsible for making all final decisions.

Try to hold your family meetings at a regular time and at an hour convenient for everyone (don't make the kids miss their Saturday morning cartoons). Also consider taking notes at your meetings: write down important information and any agreements made between family members (for example, "Debbie will do the dishes on Saturday and Sunday nights").

Try to make your family meetings a relaxed and positive experience. Spend time discussing upcoming events and plans, such as vacations. Praise each member for good behavior that week. If all goes well, your family and you will feel a little stronger and healthier at each meeting. You will likely enjoy working out your problems as a team; even if you disagree at times, you will know you are there together, building a better future.

Children under 2/2-5/6-12/Teenagers

20. Go to Family Therapy

IN THE PREVIOUS "WAY," I SUGGESTED THAT YOU hold family meetings to solve problems and encourage appropriate behavior in your child. But if you find, after several tries, that your family is unable to sit down together peacefully, unable to talk, share feelings, and work things out, then I strongly recommend that you see a family therapist.

Family therapists (also called Marriage and Family Therapists or Marriage, Family, and Child Counselors) work on improving relationships between family members. They use a variety of methods to move individuals and families in a healthier direction. They help families overcome many difficulties, including divorce trauma, parent-child conflicts, and child behavior problems. Family therapists can lower family tension and increase awareness and understanding. They can raise the self-esteem of each family member and strengthen the family's weaknesses and vulnerabilities.

I can tell you, based on my education in this field, that many serious family problems do not go away without professional help. (I define a serious problem, in general, as one that lasts six months or more, despite various efforts within the family to make it go away.) Serious family problems seem to show up in every family in one form or another, generation after generation. Most families go through years of pain and frustration before they get help—if they get help at all.

Licensed family therapists are required by law to maintain a confidential relationship with each family. This means that the therapist will not give any information about your family to anyone outside of the therapy setting (there are some exceptions to this rule). Family therapists' styles can be very different, so I recommend that you "shop around" until you find a therapist you like. Luckily, they are affordable and easy to find.

Check your local Yellow Pages Directory under Marriage and Family Therapy, Psychologists, or Mental Health Services.

Children under 2/2-5/6-12/Teenagers

THE
50 WAYS

PART THREE
Four Ways to Shape Your Child's Environment

21. Simplify Your Child's Environment

THERE ARE MANY WAYS YOU CAN CREATE AN ENVIRONMENT for your child that will encourage appropriate behavior. For example, remove items in your home that can cause your child to get into trouble. Parents with young children can consider buying unbreakable dishes and food containers. Put valued objects out of your child's reach. Make sure clothes are easy for your child to put on. (Look for clothes with large buttons, for example.) You can also provide racks and shelves low enough for your child to keep his or her important belongings on them.

Older children need a quiet, comfortable place to study. Try to provide your child with a well-lit table or desk and a safe place to keep books, schoolwork, and supplies.

When school children are not studying, they look for fun things to do. You can help by creating a game or activity closet (or other storage area) for your child. Fill the closet with your child's electronic games, board games, or puzzles. Make a place for sports equipment, including balls for football, baseball, and basketball, and be sure that everything in the closet is accessible to your child.

You can also simplify your child's clothes closet by organizing it into sections for school clothing, after-school or play clothing, and formal or Sunday clothing. For teenagers who do their own laundry, you can provide special containers for their closet or bathroom. Label the containers "White Clothes" and "Colored Clothes" to help your child sort out dirty clothes. Try to see your home through your child's eyes and ask what you can do to make his or her life easier. If you can make your child's life a little easier, chances are you will make your life easier, too.

Children under 2/2-5/6-12/Teenagers

22. Enrich Your Child's Environment

THE MORE OPPORTUNITIES YOU GIVE YOUR CHILD to behave appropriately, the less chance he or she will behave inappropriately. Try to have numerous fun, safe, and interesting play options for your child. Choose toys that are age-appropriate and designed to increase your child's creativity and self-confidence. Early childhood is the best time to develop your child's interest in reading, so don't wait for your child's schools to do the job. Create a personal library for your child, providing a balanced diet of fiction and nonfiction books, gathered from your local bookstore and public library. Then watch your child's library grow with books that he or she will treasure for a lifetime.

If possible, provide a special area or play room for your child. Whether inside or outside the house, or in the garage, in this space your child will know he or she is free to explore and create. Young children, for example, delight in a place where they can be messy and work with their favorite art materials, such as clay, paint, and crayons. Older children also appreciate a special work area—a place where they can develop their interests or hobbies, such as carpentry, playing drums, or dressmaking. In their own space children will enjoy a sense of freedom and comfort, and parents will enjoy watching their children behave well.

Children under 2/2-5/6-12/Teenagers

23. Limit Your Child's Environment

ONE WAY TO DISCOURAGE INAPPROPRIATE BEHAVIOR is to limit your child's environment. When you are away from home, avoid taking your child to places where his or her needs for food, rest, toileting, or exploration cannot be easily met. Avoid restaurants where the service is slow or the food is unfamiliar to your child. Avoid taking your child to violent or sexually explicit movies that could cause him or her to be frightened or confused.

Inside your home, you may have to limit your child's environment at certain times. For example, be aware of stereos, telephones, and video games that interfere with a child's homework time; too much distraction could cause him or her to misbehave. Bedtime can be a real nightmare for some parents. If your child has difficulty going to sleep, try to keep stimulating toys and games away from your child at bedtime. Also, don't allow your child to watch TV in the hour before his or her bedtime.

Incidentally, how many hours a day *does* your child watch TV? The average child in America spends more time watching TV than in any other single activity except sleep. By the time children become teenagers, they will have watched approximately 15,000 hours of television (Mussen, Conger, and Kagan, *Child Development and Personality*, p. 408). The good news is that certain educational programs on TV teach children appropriate behaviors, such as tolerance, cooperation, and obedience in school. These shows include "Barney and Friends," "Mister Rogers' Neighborhood," and "Sesame Street."

The bad news is that most television shows contain violence proven to be harmful to children. Studies show that the more violence a child sees on TV, the more aggressive he or she is likely to be in attitudes and behavior (McConnell, *Understanding Human Behavior*, p. 90). Children learn a variety of inappropriate behaviors from watching TV, with special lessons in how *not* to be a friendly person. They learn, for example, that fighting gets you what you want. They learn how *not* to cooperate and share with others and how *not* to use self-control.

In order to curb your child's appetite for violent TV, I recommend that you limit the quantity of TV that your child views. For example, try making a rule in your home, such as TV only one hour a day, or TV only before dinner or only on Saturday.

By manipulating your child's surroundings, both in and out of your home, you will learn to spot problem situations in advance. You will also create an environment that encourages appropriate behavior.

Children under 2/2-5/6-12/Teenagers

24. Keep Your House in Order

IMAGINE THAT YOU HAVE JUST WELCOMED A VISITOR from another country into your home. You do not know how long this visitor plans to stay with your family, but you want him or her to be as comfortable as possible. The only problem is that your visitor has difficulty speaking and understanding your language. Sound familiar? Indeed, children are a lot like foreign visitors. They are highly curious beings, vulnerable and dependent on others; they must try to get along in a strange adult world. What can you do to help your visitor-like child adjust to living in your home?

The following will give you some ideas.

Keep your house clean and neat.

I do not suggest that you spend eight hours each day scrubbing floors, but try to follow a regular cleaning schedule (I hope you will not have to do the household chores by yourself). The amount of time you spend cleaning will depend on the size of your home, but the goal is still the same—to keep the dirt and clutter from accumulating. A word about clutter. Many people, including myself, believe that "everything has its place." Don't get in the habit of leaving things out where they don't belong—they can cause accidents, get lost, or be destroyed. Make a place for things! Your child will soon learn where to find the things that he or she needs (and be less dependent on you). Remember, when your home is neat and clean and things are put back in a regular place, it is a safer and easier place for you and your child to live.

Establish regular times for routine behaviors.

Routine behaviors are the simple habits that make up our daily lives. Behaviors such as eating and sleeping are common to everyone. What are some of your child's routine behaviors? Like many parents, you may have already established a rule about dinnertime or bedtime: "Bedtime is at 8:30 P.M." Princess Diana, for example, requires her two sons, William and Harry, to write thank you notes or letters to family members and friends each night at 6:00 P.M. (Morton, *Diana: Her True Story*, p. 213).

Another great habit for parents to enforce is homework time. For example, you might say, "Homework must be done immediately after dinner," or "Homework must be done before going outside to play." As always, be consistent and ready to enforce all house rules (*see* Way 28).

By establishing regular times for some (but not all) routine behaviors, you set healthy limits for your child. You add order and regularity to your home, and, best of all, you give your child a sense of security. Your child will soon learn a certain comfort and safety that comes from knowing what to expect and when to expect it in your home.

Children under 2/2-5/6-12/Teenagers

THE
50 WAYS

PART FOUR

Sixteen Ways to Give
Your Child Consequences

GENERAL GUIDELINES

25. Set Clear Limits

YOUR HOME IS YOUR CHILD'S FIRST INTRODUCTION to the way the world works. It is a small model of the world, a miniature society. By setting limits for your child at home, you are teaching him or her that rules, laws, and restrictions exist everywhere. If your child learns to respect rules at a young age, he or she will be spared much suffering in the future. Your rules should be stated as clearly and as briefly as possible, so your child can understand and remember them. The child has to know where the line is drawn and that a negative consequence will result, as in the real world, if he or she chooses to cross the line. A negative consequence, or punishment, is defined here as any approach you use to discourage inappropriate behavior in your child. Negative consequences include ignoring the behavior (Way 1), saying "No!" to your child (Way 13) and taking away a privilege (Way 37).

On the other hand, it is important to give your child a positive consequence whenever possible if he or she stays within the line. A positive consequence is any approach or reward you use to encourage appropriate behavior in your child, for example, praise, affection, material things, or time spent with you.

By setting clear limits, you teach your child to be aware of his or her behavior, both the good and the bad.

Children under 2/2-5/6-12/Teenagers

26. Give Immediate Consequences

HUMAN BEHAVIOR IS HARD TO PREDICT and hard to control, and this is especially true of children; but we can rely on certain things. For example, we know that consequences work best when they follow the behavior immediately. Positive consequences, such as rewards, are most effective when they immediately follow appropriate behavior (*see* Way 29). Give your child immediate words of praise. Saying, "You did a good job on your homework," or "I'm proud of you for telling the truth," helps encourage such appropriate behavior in the future. By the same token, a negative consequence, such as Time Out (Way 34), should be given immediately following inappropriate behavior, if possible. Don't make excuses to avoid dealing with your child's inappropriate behavior. If your consequence is fair, reasonable, and immediate, you are doing your job well.

By giving your child immediate consequences for his or her actions, you are more likely to encourage appropriate behavior and discourage inappropriate behavior in the future.

Children under 2/2-5/6-12/Teenagers

27. Follow Through

WHICHEVER WAY YOU CHOOSE TO DISCIPLINE YOUR CHILD, you must follow through. Regardless of whether you are rewarding your child for appropriate behavior or giving a negative consequence for inappropriate behavior, do what you say you will do. If your child is under the age of two, you can follow through by using the ignoring technique (Way 1) with inappropriate behavior, such as tantrums. Be sure to take away things such as cleaning products and sharp utensils that may be harmful to your infant child.

Sometimes following through is simply a test of endurance. I counseled a mother whose ten-year-old child was giving her a lot of problems at home. She told me, for example, that he had recently thrown a plate of spaghetti onto a kitchen wall. I asked her what she did next. She replied that she immediately sent the boy off to his room with the instructions that when he came out, he would clean up the mess in the kitchen. The boy responded to Mom's instructions by staying in his room all night. Mom grew impatient and cleaned up the spaghetti. The boy learned two things from this incident: one, he can manipulate Mom, and two, he can escape his consequences. Don't give your child loopholes to avoid responsibility for his or her actions. Few loopholes exist in the real world. Teach your child to respect your words by always following through, and he or she will show you greater respect in the future.

Children under 2/2–5/6–12/Teenagers

28. Be Consistent

DISCIPLINE IS NOT POSSIBLE WITHOUT CONSISTENCY. Children learn that their behavior is appropriate or inappropriate as parents respond to their behavior with positive or negative consequences. Every time your child shows good or appropriate behavior, reward him or her in some way. Meanwhile, every time your child shows bad or inappropriate behavior, ensure a negative consequence of some kind.

Your child will likely continue to test the limits you set until you are able to respond to his or her behavior in a consistent way. In order to control your child's behavior, you must be aware of both the good and the bad, and you must constantly work to encourage the good and discourage the bad. They are equally important.

Children under 2/2-5/6-12/Teenagers

POSITIVE CONSEQUENCES

29. Give Immediate Rewards

IF YOU REWARD YOUR CHILD'S EFFORTS, he or she will be more likely to behave appropriately. And the best rewards are given immediately following the appropriate behavior—the moment you see or hear it. You have an unlimited number of immediate rewards from which to choose.

Some popular ones are candy, hugs, words of praise, snacks, toys, and money. I recommend you vary the rewards you give your child. Relying only on food rewards, for example, can cause food to be tremendously important to a child and can lead to eating problems later in life. Parents should also be wary of material rewards and use them sparingly; the more often material rewards are used, the less effective and more expensive they become.

Praise is, by far, the best reward you can give your child. Praise is so important to a child's good behavior that it should be given along with any other rewards that you use. Make it very clear to your talking-age child why he or she is being rewarded.

You might say, for example, "I liked the way you put your school books in your room when you got home today." Notice that you are pointing out to your child the specific behavior he or she did that was appropriate. I recommend that parents avoid using expressions like, "You're a good boy (girl)." Children are neither good nor bad—only their behavior is good or bad.

As I mentioned in the introduction, good discipline does two things: it eliminates the inappropriate behavior, and it encourages the appropriate behavior. And a child's appropriate behavior depends on rewards. So, reward your child's appropriate behavior—immediately, if possible—and you are likely to see more of it in the future.

Children under 2/2-5/6-12/Teenagers

30. Take Time to Play with Your Child

ONE OF THE BEST WAYS TO ENCOURAGE APPROPRIATE BEHAVIOR in your child is through the wonders of play: just you and your child, one-on-one. The possibilities are endless. Examples for infants and young children include playing peek-a-boo, patty-cake, hide 'n' seek, and dress-up or teaching your child a new song. Play with older children could involve such things as going for a picnic, riding a horse, making banana splits, visiting the puppies in a local pet store, building a snowperson, playing a board game (such as Scrabble or Monopoly), or shopping at the local mall.

Parent-child play is important for a variety of reasons. First, it provides a time when you can give your child positive attention. Children, especially very young children, need an abundance of positive attention from their parents. Too often children act out inappropriately (and suffer painful consequences) in order to satisfy their basic need for attention.

Playtime (or recreation time) with your child is also a way to encourage *healthy* play activities. For example, if you want your child to spend more time outdoors, you could suggest a game of catch or basketball.

Best of all, parent-child play is a way to build your child's self-esteem—and a healthy self-esteem is central to your child's personal happiness, success in school, and achievement in later life.

So, take time out regularly to have fun with your child, and when you do, keep these things in mind:

- **Make sure the activities you do together are appropriate for your child's age and size.**

- **Try to choose play activities that give your child an opportunity to show off his or her talents, skills, and uniqueness.**

- **Avoid criticizing your child's behavior during playtime; this is the time to give lots of praise and encouragement.**

Playing with your child is an easy way to say, "I love you. You are important to me." It is another way to help your child feel good inside, so that he or she will do good things in the future.

Children under 2/2-5/6-12/Teenagers

31. Promise a Future Reward

ANOTHER WAY TO ENCOURAGE APPROPRIATE BEHAVIOR in your child is to offer a future reward (an immediate reward is the best reward, but a future reward can also be effective). The reward can be large or small. I knew a teenage girl whose parents promised her a large sum of money if she did not touch drugs or alcohol before the age of 21. While most parents cannot offer their children large dollar rewards, even small amounts of money can be used to reinforce a child's good behavior. Giving your child an allowance at the end of the week, for example, is a great way to encourage him or her to do weekly chores.

Besides money, you can use many other important things of value to your child as future rewards. Perhaps you could promise your child an afternoon alone with you at home, playing a favorite game, or you could take a trip somewhere—to the beach, to the park, or to see a movie. Sometimes a child has special people, such as a grandma or grandpa, and a visit to see them would be a nice reward for appropriate behavior. Other rewards to promise include a new toy, a book, a special dessert, extra TV time, or playtime.

Try to use the resources you have right now to shape your child's behavior in a positive way. Rather than giving your child whatever he or she wants, whenever he or she wants it, teach your child responsibility and self-control. Teach your child how to earn rewards for appropriate behavior. Give your child the motivation to behave well by rewarding good behavior.

Children 2-5/6-12/Teenagers

32. Use a Token Reward System

A TOKEN REWARD SYSTEM CAN BE A FUN AND EASY WAY to help a child gain control of his or her behavior. Your child will be attracted to the interesting chart you make and the reward he or she can earn for appropriate behavior. And you will look forward to watching your child's behavior improve day by day. When using this system, always make sure that you do not reinforce a "not" (for example, *not* hitting sibling), but rather reinforce the appropriate behavior (for example, playing quietly with sibling). Following are the four steps of the Token Reward System.

In Step 1, make a behavior chart.

Think of the two or three most troublesome behaviors your child exhibits. (You can make a chart for any number of behaviors, but I suggest that you limit the number to three or less, so that your child will not feel overwhelmed with pressure to change.) You may, for example, want your child to clean his or her room or stop teasing a younger brother or sister. Maybe your child has been getting in trouble at school for turning in late homework assignments, and you want the schoolwork done on time. Whatever behaviors you choose, list them vertically (up and down) on a large piece of paper (you can find colored construction paper at your local art supply store). At the top of the chart, write the days of the week horizontally. Now, in a gridlike fashion, draw vertical and horizontal lines across the chart, so that the days of the week correspond with each behavior listed (*see* Picture A).

The Token Reward System

Picture A

APPROPRIATE BEHAVIOR	MON	TUES	WED	THUR	FRI	SAT	SUN	TOTAL
Cleans room								
Plays quietly with sibling								
Finishes homework on time*								
TOTAL NUMBER OF TOKENS EARNED (AFTER 1 WEEK) =								

Picture B

APPROPRIATE BEHAVIOR	MON	TUES	WED	THUR	FRI	SAT	SUN	TOTAL
Cleans room		X		X	X	X	X	5
Plays quietly with sibling	X		X	X	X		X	5
Finishes homework on time*	X	X		X	X			8
TOTAL NUMBER OF TOKENS EARNED (AFTER 1 WEEK) = 18								

*Each "X" in this column equals 2 tokens.

In Step 2, select a token.

A token should be something small, durable, and lightweight—such things as poker chips and paper money work well. You will give your child a token at the end of each day if he or she demonstrates the desirable behavior (plays quietly with sibling, cleans room, completes homework on time, etc.).

In Step 3, decide how many tokens each appropriate behavior is worth.

For example, tell your child that he or she will receive one token for each day he or she plays quietly with sister or brother, one token if he or she cleans the room, and two tokens if he or she finishes all homework on schedule.

In Step 4, choose a reward.

Sit down with your child and decide on a fair reward for his or her total effort and cooperation. You might decide, if you live in southern California, that fifty tokens earned equals a trip to Disneyland. Other possible rewards include a special dinner for your child, a new game or toy, an article of clothing, or an ice-cream party with friends.

At this point, you are ready to begin using the Token Reward System. Talk to your child and set up a starting point and date (for example, Monday morning at 8:00 A.M.). Each day, watch your child to see whether he or she displays the correct chart behavior(s). At the end of the day, give your child the number of tokens earned. Always record the results on your chart: put an "X" in the corresponding box if your child receives any tokens (*see* Picture B). You can find the total number of tokens your child earned by adding up the tokens at the end of each column.

The Behavior Chart is a way for you to monitor your child's appropriate behavior—and when your chart is used up, simply replace it with a new one. (**A word of caution:** Give your child at least one week to become familiar with the Token Reward System. Don't expect overnight results.)

As your child's behavior improves, you can update the chart by removing old problem behaviors from the list and adding new ones. If you have other children living at home, consider putting them on the chart as well and giving them tokens for appropriate behavior.

The best time to end the Token Reward System is when your child exhibits the appropriate behavior(s) on a regular basis. At this time, gradually wean your child away from the token rewards. You can do this by giving your child less tokens for the same behavior, or you can give the tokens out less frequently, for example, once a week instead of every day. Eventually you can phase the tokens out completely.

The main advantage of the Token Reward System is that it uses a positive approach to discipline. You will not have to scold or punish your child for inappropriate behavior—he or she will simply not get any tokens for the day. Your child will likely try harder tomorrow.

Children 6–12/Teenagers

NEGATIVE CONSEQUENCES

33. Learn the Holding Technique

USING THE HOLDING TECHNIQUE, a parent will physically restrain a child. *This technique should not be painful to the child in any way.* The Holding Technique requires you to wrap your fully extended arms around your child, thereby hindering his or her physical movement. *The child's breathing should be normal at all times.* You can stand with your child or carry the child to a chair and hold him or her there.

The Holding Technique can be used most appropriately as a means of protecting small children from hazardous situations—for example, if a child tries to approach a stray dog or run into the street. In such situations, if the child fails to respond to the parent's verbal warning, the consequences can be dangerous: the child can be bitten by the dog or run over by a car. By using the Holding Technique the parent can protect the child quickly and effectively.

The same is true for less dramatic, yet potentially dangerous, situations. For example, a parent firmly asks a child to stop a certain behavior, such as running through the house, but the child ignores the parent and continues with the behavior. In this case, the child might be careless and hurt him or herself by tripping over something, falling down the stairs, or hitting a wall. Therefore, after unsuccessfully trying to stop the child's behavior verbally, the parent can then use the Holding Technique to restrain the child until the child agrees to stop the original behavior. Once the parent sets the child free, the child may resume the inappropriate behavior. (This is the child's natural way of testing your effectiveness as a parent, so be ready to restrain him or her again.)

Always remember to stay calm and in control of your behavior whenever you use the Holding Technique. This will help your child gain control of his or her behavior. By remaining calm you will also avoid escalating a protective situation into one of physical conflict.

Children 2–5

34. Use Time Outs

TIME OUT IS A MILD FORM OF PUNISHMENT that can be very effective. If used properly, it teaches your child to gain control of his or her behavior. As adults, we take self-control for granted, but it is an extremely important and challenging task that we first face as children. In Time Out, you remove your child immediately from the "scene of the crime," or the place where the inappropriate behavior is occurring, and put him or her in an isolated place.

The ideal place for a Time Out is a corner space in your home or a small room where the child cannot be stimulated by things in his or her environment, such as TV, toys, games, or other children. (Chairs are acceptable to use if your child would prefer to sit during a Time Out.) Many parents send their children to their rooms when they behave badly. I do not recommend this for two reasons. First, a child's room is usually filled with a lot of fun, stimulating activities. This makes it difficult for the child to settle down and think about his or her misbehavior. Second, a child's room (ideally) should be a personal sanctuary—the place where he or she can go for comfort and pleasure. Children should not associate their bedroom with punishment in any way.

Also, *never* use a Time Out place, such as a closet or other small, dark place, that is frightening to your child. If your child is uncomfortable or afraid, he or she will be thinking about those feelings rather than the inappropriate behavior. Use of such places is a form of child abuse and can lead to lasting psychological harm.

Another important thing to consider is how long you will keep your child in Time Out. The general rule is that the child's age equals the number of minutes in Time Out. For example:

Age five years = five minutes
Age six years = six minutes
Age ten years = ten minutes

Note: Never impose Time Outs on children under the age of two years.

Time Outs are especially useful when children are acting out or behaving in a destructive way. To further understand how Time Outs work, let's imagine that a boy, age six, is cruelly teasing another child, perhaps a younger sibling. The parent in this case asks the boy to leave the other child alone, but he continues with the inappropriate behavior. At this point, the parent should calmly tell the boy that it is time to take a short Time Out, and then lead him to the Time Out spot or room in the home. The child may not go willingly, so the parent must be prepared to drag or carry him (without harm) as he kicks and screams. The parent should make it clear to the boy that he will be in Time Out for a short period, and during that time, he must calm down and get control of his behavior. (Many parents find it helpful to set a timer with a buzzer to keep track of the minutes.) Once the child has served his Time Out, the parent should be prepared to send him back, as many times as necessary, the moment he acts out again.

Time Out can also be used away from home. You can call Time Out if your child becomes disobedient or disruptive in a public place, such as a grocery store, shopping mall, or restaurant. Calmly tell your child that it is time for a Time Out and walk him or her to your car (you can carry the child if he or she is under the age of five).

Stay with your child in the car. Follow the general rule and do the recommended number of Time Out minutes with your child. Sit quietly in the car; your child can read, play silently, or rest.

Hint: If your child is extremely resistant to taking a Time Out, try using the ignoring technique (Way 1), and then take a half hour off your child's bedtime. Explain to your child at bedtime that because he or she refused to take a Time Out today, then he or she must go to bed a half hour earlier tonight.

As your child learns the difficult task of self-control, you should set a good example. The more self-control you show during the Time Out procedure, the faster your child will learn to control his or her behavior.
Children 2-5/6-12

35. Take Away Things that Are Misused

SCHOOL TEACHERS ARE FAMOUS FOR TAKING THINGS from children as a way to stop inappropriate behavior in the classroom. They have been known to take from students things such as chewing gum, candy, personal notes and letters, comic books, and fashion magazines, because these things disrupt a class and prevent children from learning. When your child misuses something, whatever it is, try taking it away. If your child is under the age of two, you may have to take an item or belonging away until he or she is old enough to understand how to use it properly. (In this case, the purpose of taking something away is not to punish the child, but simply to protect him or her and also the possession.) I suggest taking a possession away for one day if the child is two to five years old, two days if the child is six to twelve years old, and one week if the child is a teenager. Explain clearly to your child the reason for taking away his or her possession and for how long you will keep it.

Never punish children by depriving them of their basic human needs for good health and safety. (For example, never take away a child's food, shelter, or clothing.) You can take things away from your child in a variety of situations to stop inappropriate behavior. Here are some examples:

- Take away a child's toy if he or she uses it to hit others.

- Take away a child's video game if he or she stays up all night playing with it.

- Take away a child's pet animal (and give it to an adult friend to hold) if he or she does not properly care for it.

- Take away a child's form of transportation (skateboard, bike, rollerskates, and the like) if he or she goes to forbidden places.

Of course, you will return all of these things, as a teacher would, with the understanding that the inappropriate behavior should not occur again. And if it does, you must be ready to deprive your child again, as many times as necessary, until the inappropriate behavior stops.

Children under 2/2–5/6–12/Teenagers

36. Let Your Child Make Restitution for Inappropriate Behavior

RESTITUTION MEANS TO REPLACE OR MAKE UP for something that has been damaged, lost, or taken away. When a boy throws a baseball through a glass window, and his father responds with the words, "You're going to pay for that broken window out of your allowance money, young man," the father is asking his son to make restitution for his behavior.

Children can make restitution in various ways: through money (as in the example of the baseball); through replacement of lost items; through deeds (they can do extra chores around the house); and through words (they can restore hurt feelings with such words as, "I'm sorry").

A parent, for example, may ask a child to apologize to others when the child has behaved in an unfair or insensitive way. A friend of mine gave me a wonderful example of how her mother used restitution in her home while she was growing up. Apparently, whenever my friend was caught calling her brother a cruel name, she was given the consequence of saying five nice things to him. (Fortunately, the restitution rule applied to him as well.) She might say, for example, "You have nice hair," "You are a good dancer," or "You are very smart."

My friend told me how truly difficult and distasteful it was to give out those compliments to her brother. Nevertheless, she did it. I applaud my friend's mother, who clearly understood the importance of using restitution as a means of restoring hurt feelings and self-esteem.

Through restitution, children learn to take responsibility for

their behavior. They learn how to redeem themselves, both in their own eyes and in the eyes of their parents.
Children 2-5/6-12/Teenagers

37. Take Away a Privilege

"GROUNDING" IS A POPULAR CONSEQUENCE parents give children today. Every time you ground your child, you take away a privilege—the privilege to participate in recreational activities outside the home. Other privileges you can take away from your child include the use of video games, the telephone or television, or transportation, such as rollerskates, skateboards, bicycles, and the family car (if your child can drive). As with other negative consequences, take away a privilege for a *reasonable* period of time. I recommend taking a privilege away for only one day if a child is two to five years old, two days for children ages six to twelve, and one week for teenagers. Make sure your child understands how long the privilege will be taken away and the reason for the negative consequence. Explain why his or her behavior was inappropriate. Be specific.

Never punish a child by taking away his or her food. (In this country, food, at least for children, is a right, not a privilege.) I would also caution parents who take away a child's allowance money as a negative consequence. I do not consider an allowance to be a privilege, because children, in most cases, do work (chores) for their money each week. An allowance is more of a reward for their effort. I believe if children do their work, they should receive their allowance, if that is the deal to which you agreed. If it works, I would not interfere with it!

However, with a privilege, there is no contract. Privileges are the things in your child's life that he or she gets without any real effort. You are free to take them away at any time! You may have to experiment to see what works as an effective consequence for your child.

Hint: If the inappropriate behavior continues, try taking away a different privilege. The important thing, once again, is that you enforce your decision to take away a privilege; so be prepared to remove a TV set from a room or hide a skateboard or video game if necessary.

Children 2–5/6–12/Teenagers

38. Use Natural Consequences

A NATURAL CONSEQUENCE is simply the unavoidable consequence of a child's inappropriate behavior. For example, if a child refuses to eat dinner, he or she will feel hungry, and the child who eats too much candy may get a stomach ache. A child who stays up late to watch a scary movie on TV might have nightmares, and the child who forgets to take his or her sweater to school may get cold. If a child leaves his or her bicycle outside all night, two natural consequences may occur. First, the bike could rust in bad weather, and second, the bike could get stolen.

What would be the natural consequence if a child acts carelessly and breaks a toy? The natural consequence is that the child can no longer play with that toy. In this case, a good response from a parent would be, "Gee, it's a shame you broke your toy. I know how much you liked to play with it. I'm sure you will take better care of your things in the future."

Natural consequences are usually so powerful that parents

do not have to punish or scold a child further. Try to find the natural consequence in your child's inappropriate behavior and use it whenever possible. It is an easy way to teach your child how to be more aware of his or her behavior and more responsible as a person.

Children 2-5/6-12/Teenagers

39. Give Fair Consequences

WHEN YOU USE FAIR CONSEQUENCES, YOU GIVE YOUR CHILD an opportunity to decide on the consequence for his or her inappropriate behavior. Children generally look forward to this approach and consider it to be fair because they get to choose their own negative consequence. As a parent, you will appreciate knowing that your child is willing to accept responsibility for his or her behavior. In this approach, you simply ask your child to take some time to think about his or her actions, and then decide on a fair consequence. However, you must overrule any unreasonable consequence your child offers (young children have a tendency to be harsh self-disciplinarians).

An *unfair* consequence is one that is inappropriate for the child's age and stage of development. An unfair consequence is overly harsh and capable of causing great emotional and/or physical suffering to the child. Numerous hours of Time Out, the destruction of a child's favorite toy or other possession, and any form of corporal punishment are unfair consequences.

By contrast, a *fair* consequence is a punishment that "fits the crime," so to speak. It also takes into consideration the child's age and stage of development. Fair consequences include enforcing Time Out correctly (Way 34), taking something away that is misused (Way 35), using restitution (Way 36), and taking away a privilege (Way 37). Here are some specific examples:

• **Preschool-age:**
   Behavior: Child hits another child
   Fair Consequence: Child must apologize to other child

   Behavior: Child throws food at dinner table
   Fair Consequence: Time Out

• **School-age:**
   Behavior: Child ignores homework assignment
   Fair Consequence: Child loses TV privilege for two days

   Behavior: Child leaves rollerskates outside all night
   Fair Consequence: Child loses rollerskate privileges for two days

• **Teenagers**
   Behavior: Child refuses to come to dinner
   Fair Consequence: Child must make his or her own dinner

   Behavior: Child comes home past curfew
   Fair Consequence: Child loses phone privilege for one week

While I would not recommend using this approach on a regular basis, I do know that it can be effective. The experience can be somewhat positive for your child and develop his or her sense of responsibility and fairness for the future.

Children 2-5/6-12/Teenagers

40. Give Logical Consequences

IN THIS APPROACH, parents are asked to think of a logical, reasonable consequence that may follow the child's inappropriate behavior. The Logical Consequences approach is a truly extraordinary form of discipline because it teaches children responsibility and self-control. When using this approach, parents give children the option of cooperating or suffering the consequences of their actions. For example:

- **If a child refuses to eat dinner...**
  the child cannot have dessert.
- **If a child is being loud and disruptive...**
  the child must go to another room.
- **If a child does not do his or her chores...**
  the child does not receive his or her allowance.

Ideally, the parent should get the child's agreement when arranging the logical consequence. That way, the child will be fully aware that he or she has the choice to alter the consequences of their actions. The following is an example of a logical consequence that can be used with an older child:

- **A teenager leaves dirty cloths scattered all over the bedroom. The parent tells the teenager, "I am too busy to pick up your dirty clothes every day. If you don't put your clothes in the clothes hamper, they will not get washed."**

You should not yell or nag the child—the consequence should be enough to motivate the child to cooperate. Your tone of voice should be calm and matter-of-fact when using this approach. Here are some guidelines to remember:

- **Make clear to your child what you expect from his or her behavior.**
- **Let your child take responsibility for the choices he or she makes.**
- *Always* **follow through with the consequence.**

Unlike natural consequences, logical consequences are planned: you are responsible for creating a *fair* and *appropriate* consequence for your child. Parenting experts recommend this approach because, when used correctly, it is safe and effective. It also contains a wonderful built-in lesson for your child: you not only discourage the inappropriate behavior, but also encourage the appropriate behavior.

Hint: If you find that your consequence is not producing the desired results, try using another type of logical consequence, such as Time Out (Way 34), Restriction (Way 36), or Taking Away a Privilege (Way 37).

Children 2–5/6–12/Teenagers

THE
50 WAYS
PART FIVE
Ten Ways to Meet Your
Needs as a Parent

41. Call Someone

ONE HUNDRED YEARS AGO YOU WERE LIKELY to be surrounded by extended family members—uncles, aunts, parents, and cousins—who lived either with you or close by. These caring people provided each other with many things, including emotional support when times were hard. Today, however, life is very different. Parents frequently find themselves alone and overwhelmed with the difficult task of raising children.

Support systems are necessary for your physical and emotional well-being. In fact, I cannot overemphasize the importance of having a large number of support systems in your life. A support system can be a relative, someone you know from a church, club, or other social organization, a member of a self-help group to which you belong, a coworker, a neighbor, an old or a new friend. Good support systems come in many shapes and sizes, but I think all of them meet the following standards:

- **They are available to you most hours of the day or night.**

- **They are good listeners. They won't interrupt you. They won't criticize you. They will let you vent your anger, frustration, fear, and pain over the phone.**

- **They won't ask you for anything other than that you be there for them in the same way.**

- **They genuinely make you feel better.**

Many parents find it comforting to talk to someone on a crisis hotline. Hotline workers are caring people (usually trained volunteers and counselors) who can really listen to you and give you the support you need. Some hotlines are available twenty-four hours a day.

To find the crisis hotline near you, dial your operator or 411 for information. You can also check your Yellow Pages Phone Directory under the listings for Social Service Organizations or Mental Health Services to locate support services available in your area. I encourage you to make a list of the support systems you have in your life right now. Keep this list of names and phone numbers by your telephone at all times. Meanwhile, continue to seek out friends and build your support systems for the future. This way, you will never have to go through a crisis alone.

42. Learn to Relax

THERE IS STRESS IN ALMOST EVERYTHING YOU DO. You will experience stress if you move to a new home, get a new job, or change your eating or sleeping habits. Even going on vacation is stressful. And by now, you are familiar with the stress involved in raising a child. What do you do with the stress that builds up in your everyday life?

People use good and bad ways to reduce stress and tension. Bad ways include overeating, smoking, drinking alcohol, yelling, and fighting. Good ways include dancing, bowling and other recreational activities, doing exercises such as swimming or walking, getting a body massage, spending time with a favorite animal, or listening to music. I recommend that you create a special place to relax in your home or at work (if you have a job outside the home). Consider such things as lighting, sounds, color, and chairs, and add whatever you can to create a relaxed atmosphere. This could be the place you go for peace and comfort.

One of the best ways to reduce stress in your life is by practicing total relaxation exercises, which include progressive muscle relaxation, meditation (used around the world), and visualization. These exercises are effective because they allow you to relax your mind and body completely—something you can't do even in your sleep. Total relaxation exercises may sound complicated, but they are actually very easy to learn, and they begin to work in about sixty seconds (*see* Suggested Readings and Referral Information on page 101 for more information about these exercises). Following is a brief summary of possible relaxation exercises.

Progressive Muscle Relaxation

Step 1: Find a quiet, peaceful place, such as a bedroom, den, office, or grassy spot under a tree.

Step 2: Choose a comfortable position. You may lie down or sit in a chair for this exercise.

Step 3: Take deep breaths using your diaphragm. Breathe slowly and maintain a steady rhythm.

Step 4: Concentrate on each muscle group, beginning with your toes and working your way up. Speak slowly and monotonously. For example, you might say to yourself, "My toes are tingling. I feel my toes becoming numb." When one area of your body is completely relaxed, move on to the next. Use words like "calm" and "heavy" and "warm" to move yourself into a deeper state of relaxation. After you have relaxed your entire body, you can remain in this peaceful state for several minutes.

Meditation

Step 1: Find a quiet, peaceful place, such as a bedroom, den, office, or grassy spot under a tree.

Step 2: Sit in a comfortable position for this exercise. Sit cross-legged on a cushion or, if you prefer, sit on a chair in a regular sitting position.

Step 3: Take deep breaths using your diaphragm. Breathe slowly and maintain a steady rhythm.

Step 4: Maintain a passive attitude. Keep your mind as free and clear as possible. Avoid any distracting thoughts.

Step 5: Focus on a mental "object," such as a sound or syllable, word or phrase. A popular sound that is used in meditation is "Om." Concentrate solely on the object you selected and repeat it each time you exhale. Continue this exercise for about twenty minutes. Although some objects may have religious meaning, meditation is *not* a religion or philosophy and can be used by anyone to achieve a greater sense of awareness, inner peace, and relaxation.

Visualization

Step 1: Find a quiet, peaceful place, such as a bedroom, den, office, or grassy spot under a tree.

Step 2: Choose a comfortable position. You may lie down or sit in a chair for this exercise.

Step 3: Take deep breaths using your diaphragm. Breathe slowly and maintain a steady rhythm.

Step 4: Choose an image or mental picture that gives you a sense of pleasure and comfort. The image you choose will depend on your interests and personality. For example, if you enjoy camping and hiking, you might visualize yourself lying on a mountain, looking up at the stars. Hold that image for a moment, then create a moving picture in your mind. See yourself lying peacefully under the stars on a warm summer night. Try to experience every sensation: feel the earth beneath you, smell the flowers, hear the crickets. As you enjoy this lovely outdoor scene, you might say to yourself, "The air is clear and easy to breathe. I feel the tension leaving my body and disappearing into the darkness." Take about twenty minutes to guide yourself into a deeper and deeper state of relaxation. Enjoy the feeling of peace, happiness, and tranquility that comes through visualization.

For years, doctors have warned us that stress is bad for our health; I think stress is bad for our family too. Our relationships suffer when we get "stressed out" and irritable. Stress has a way of taking over our life and making us feel out of control. It is very important for you to have a regular and effective way to relax. Not only will you feel better physically, but you will also do your job as a parent better.

43. Keep a Family Calendar

A FAMILY CALENDAR IS AN EFFECTIVE WAY for you to manage your time and your family. It is affordable and easy to use—simply attach a standard-sized calendar to a wall, door, or refrigerator in your home.

Start your calendar by writing down important upcoming events or activities for the month. Include doctor appointments, birthdays, and family vacations. Next, you can add the various weekly activities of each family member. For example, if your child attends day care, swimming lessons, or Boy Scout or Girl Scout meetings, write them down. Does your family attend a church or temple? If so, write it down.

What other responsibilities and commitments do you (and your partner) have each week? If you have a job outside the home, you can write down any nights you work late.

Now take a look at the calendar and decide how you want to spend the remaining time and days of the month. I highly recommend that you schedule time for yourself—this will be your time to do whatever you wish without feeling guilty, time to be responsible only for yourself. You should also schedule some time (other than sleeping) to be alone with your partner each week. When you nurture your marriage or couple relationship, it benefits your family as a whole.

Finally, set aside some time to be alone with your child. If you have more than one child, set aside time for each child. One parent told me that she and her husband came up with a rotation plan that works with their four children. Each night they allow one of their children to stay up an extra fifteen minutes past bedtime just to be with Mom and Dad. This is a great approach for building a child's self-esteem; Mom and Dad can show their children that they are loved equally, but at the same time, each child feels special during his or her fifteen minutes.

The family calendar is another way for you to reduce stress and conflict in your home by helping you organize important family activities. The calendar will help you balance your time and energy so that you can do the things you need to do: take care of your home, take care of your family, and above all, take care of yourself.

44. Form a Support Group of Your Own

SELF-HELP GROUPS ARE EXTREMELY POPULAR because they work. Thousands of self-help support groups throughout the country welcome adults (single, married, or divorced), parents, and seniors. In each of these groups, individuals come together because they share a similar experience, common interest, or goal. People in support groups generally meet on a regular basis to provide emotional support and exchange information. Each group has its own advantages. For example, in a Parents' Group you may be able to help other families by sharing your experience, and you are likely to meet new friends in your community. You do not have to be a professional of any kind to start your own Parents' Group. You need only be a caring person, willing to take the time to organize the group.

There are different ways to start a group. You can use word of mouth or attach flyers to bulletin boards in your area. You can advertise in a local newspaper. As the organizer of a Parents' Group, you must consider the following:

- How many people do you want in your group?

- Do you want the group open to men and women?

- Will you allow children to attend the group meetings?

- Will you collect any dues from members to cover the cost of refreshments or materials you may have to buy?

- Where will you hold the group meetings? Your house? A neighbor's house? A local school? A park? A church?

- When do you want your group to meet?

- How long should the meetings be? (Parent support groups usually meet one day a week for about one to one-and-a-half hours.)

- Will your group be ongoing, or will it be offered for a limited number of weeks?

- Do you want group discussions to be private and confidential? If so, you can ask each member to make a verbal (but nonlegal) agreement to respect the privacy of the group and refrain from discussing group matters outside the group.

- Do you want to be the group leader as well as the group organizer?

As a group leader, you must decide whether to plan group meetings ahead of time or just get together when problems or parenting issues arise. If you choose to plan each group meeting, you can write out some questions for the group to discuss, or you can choose to assign a parenting book to to the group to discuss at a future meeting.

Remember that as a group leader, you are not there to teach, but simply to encourage other members to open up and share their feelings and experiences. Try to create a caring, trusting, and supportive atmosphere in your group. Members will soon learn that the group is a safe place to give and take freely, a place where each of you can develop your confidence as a person and your skills as a parent.

45. Don't Undermine Your Partner's Authority—and Don't Let Your Partner Undermine Yours

IF YOU ARE RAISING CHILDREN IN A TWO-PARENT HOUSEHOLD, support your partner's attempts to be an effective parent. Whether you agree or disagree with your partner's way of handling a problem situation, you should try, as parents, to maintain a united front when facing your child. The time to disagree with your partner's decision or behavior toward your child is when the two of you are alone and you are able to speak to each other in a calm, clear way.

Take time out regularly with your partner to discuss decisions about your child. It is then that you should express your thoughts about discipline matters and set up any ground rules you think are necessary when it comes to raising your child. I advise all couples to agree on the following rule: *The parent who is first aware of the inappropriate behavior must deal with it.* Too often one parent will say, "Wait until your father or mother gets home and hears what you did . . . ." This approach is faulty for various reasons. One parent is put in the "bad guy" position; he or she is the feared parent, the powerful discipline enforcer. Meanwhile, the other parent is viewed by the child as weak and ineffective, unable to function independently. These extreme images of Mom and Dad are unhealthy for a child. *Both parents should be equally effective in their ability to control their child's behavior.* In other words, never take away your partner's power as a parent, and never give away your power. Children will often look for a weak parent to control or manipulate, so you and your partner must act as a strong and equal team.

Also, whenever you face a big decision about your child, try to discuss the situation with your partner in advance. For example, if your child asks you whether he or she can go on a weekend trip with friends, a good first response would be a neutral one: "I will talk to your father (mother) about the trip, and we will give you our decision as soon as possible." In this way, your child knows that both parents will make the decision and uphold it 100 percent, leaving no room for manipulation.

Discipline is easier when you work together and support your partner's decisions. Your child will learn to respect both parents equally and no longer divide you into "the good," "the bad," "the strong," and "the weak."

46. Give Yourself Positive Affirmations

IF YOU ARE A TYPICAL PARENT, you can feel overwhelmed at times with the demands of raising a child. You can feel powerless over certain situations in your home; you can feel overworked and unappreciated. You can find yourself feeling so frustrated and angry at your child, you will wonder why you ever wanted to be a parent in the first place. These are all normal feelings that parents go through, and you can cope with these feelings in many ways.

Earlier in this book, I recommended that you call someone for extra support or do a relaxation exercise (Ways 41 and 42). You can also give yourself positive affirmations. Positive affirmations are the friendly, supportive things that you say to yourself. Here are some examples:

- I like myself.

- I am doing the best that I can.

- I forgive myself for the mistakes I made in the past.

- There is nothing wrong with making mistakes—they are simply lessons that need to be learned.

- I can make decisions for myself.

- I can control my anger.

Positive affirmations are very personal. You can decide what words give you the most hope and comfort. You should take a few minutes right now to write down some positive self affirmations. Sometimes it helps to make a list of your strengths as a person. For example:

- **I am a good friend to others.**

- **I am a hard worker.**

- **I am a responsible single parent.**

Positive affirmations can be used any time. Some people repeat a few favorite affirmations to themselves in the morning or before they go to bed at night. Try to give yourself positive affirmations every day. I think you will find the words comforting and useful to you as a parent. These are the words that will keep you going when you are down, the "self-talk" you can use to build yourself up and make yourself strong again.

47. Make Peace with Your Anger

MANY PEOPLE GROW UP IN FAMILIES with strict rules about what they can and cannot say. They are told, for example, "If you don't have something nice to say, don't say anything at all." And so they learn at an early age that it is not okay to be angry, and that to live in their family, they must bottle up their anger inside. The problem with this approach is that people can only bottle up their anger for so long until they eventually explode, venting their anger everywhere in a sadly destructive and uncontrollable way. One of the challenges, then, of being a human being and gentle disciplinarian is to learn how to express anger constructively, to communicate with others, and especially with children, in a sensitive and effective way. To do this, we must first understand the "nature of the beast," so let's discover what really lies behind this powerful and threatening emotion.

Anger is like one of those scary rubber monster masks, the kind children wear at Halloween. If we looked beneath the mask, we might find a vulnerable and sensitive being, someone who is feeling hurt or afraid or confused. But we would never know this, because all we see is the mask. Anger is the mask we sometimes wear to hide our true feelings. It is a defense, a way for us to avoid certain painful feelings, such as guilt or powerlessness or fear. Anger is also a choice, which means that we can choose whether to wear the mask.

The first step, then, in making peace with your anger is to be willing to take off the mask and let others know how you really feel. I do not encourage you to call names, to blame, or to attack others in any way—revealing your anger is not an opportunity to be verbally abusive. Rather, I suggest that you understand, accept, and reveal to others the feelings behind your anger, the feelings of pain and hurt.

Sometimes we understand our pain instantly. For example: "I am hurt that you forgot my birthday. It makes me think I'm not important to you." Other times, you need more time to uncover the feelings behind our anger. For example: "My mother-in-law moved in and she's driving me crazy! I don't know why she bugs me so much."

You may find it helpful to write down your thoughts and feelings. A personal journal, for example, can be a safe place to explore your anger and, hopefully, understand it better. Here are some questions to consider the next time you feel yourself becoming angry:

- **Are you interpreting the situation correctly?**

- **Are you saying "No" to others and setting limits so they cannot take advantage of you?**

- **Are you being realistic in your expectations of others? Of yourself?**

- **Are you expecting others to "read" your mind and know what you want and need?**

Most of us are aware of the physiological signs of anger: our faces get red, our breathing becomes heavy, we may begin to sweat or feel a pain in our stomach. But the truth is, our anger is controlled by our thoughts, by how we think about a person or situation. And through our thinking, we can make ourselves more or less angry. For example:

(Thought to **increase** anger): "My boss is such a jerk for making me work on Saturday!"

(Thought to **decrease** anger): "My boss is probably short-staffed right now and really needs my help."

Learning how to feed yourself healthy thoughts—thoughts to decrease your anger—is important for making peace with your anger.

As you can see from the previous example, anger is basically a conflict of needs. We become angry when we think that someone or something is interfering with what we want or need. Needs or wants can be large (such as love, comfort, and security) or small. Children, for example, will fight over who gets the bigger piece of cake. Whole countries will go to war over a piece of land. As I sit here and write, my cat is trying to get my attention (his wants, needs). I feel myself becoming angry because I want to be left alone to work on this book (my wants, needs).

Whether we are talking about a desire for food, attention, or homeland, anger is about individuals competing (and sometimes coming into conflict) over what they want and what they need. Try to avoid thinking in terms of right or wrong. Try to avoid thinking that others are deliberately trying to hurt you or undermine your happiness (this is rarely, if ever, the case). Instead, think about anger as a conflict of needs.

Conflicts will occur constantly throughout your life, so to have a sound problem-solving strategy is important. Fortunately, many books are available to teach you how to improve your communication and problem-solving skills. I recommend *When Anger Hurts: Quieting the Storm Within,* by McKay, Rogers, and McKay.

I have also put together my own list of general guidelines to follow whenever you are trying to resolve a conflict—and trying to avoid an angry outburst—in your home:

- **Focus on one conflict or problem at a time.**

- **Choose an appropriate time—don't try to solve a serious problem when you are tired or angry.**

- If possible, talk directly to the person with whom you have the problem.

- Express your feelings.

- Express your needs to the other person in a clear and simple way.

- **Be very specific about what you want the other person to do or not do.** What about their behavior do you want to change? Example: "I want you to make your bed every day."

- **Use "I" statements.** Example: "I am having a difficult time understanding you. Please stop yelling."

- **Use "reflective listening."** Repeat back what you hear the other person saying. Example: "I hear you saying that you are tired, and you feel overworked."

- **Know when to take a break.** If you feel your anger escalating, take an adult Time Out. (Leave the room, take a walk, do a relaxation exercise. Agree with your partner or child to separate for a period of time—about one hour.) Come back when you are ready to talk, not fight.

- **Don't attack or blame the other person.**

- Focus on compromise; look for solutions.

To resolve conflicts with others in a nonaggressive way, you must be able to control your anger. For many people, this seems to be a difficult, if not impossible, task. These people grew up in families where feelings were not openly expressed and angry outbursts were common. These people may have experienced emotional, physical, or sexual abuse as children and have unresolved anger that they still carry with them as adults.

The physical and emotional effects from constant or extreme feelings of anger can be devastating. Anger can undermine a person's most important relationships by creating an atmosphere of tension, fear, and distrust; it can leave a person feeling lonely and isolated. Anger can also destroy a person's physical health. Chronic anger has been linked to severe headaches, body rashes, stomach ulcers, and heart disease. If you have difficulty controlling your anger, help is available. I have put together a list of options for you; please try as many as possible.

- **Attend classes or workshops in anger management.**

- **Join an anger support group.** (Anger support groups can usually be found by contacting the mental health services in your area.)

- **Talk to a psychotherapist.**

- **Check your local bookstore or public library for books on anger management, problem-solving skills, or stress reduction** (*see* Suggested Readings and Referral Information, page 101).

Making peace with your anger is about looking at yourself and taking responsibility for your anger. It is knowing that you have wants and needs and learning how to express these wants and needs to others in a way that they can understand. Most of all, it is about having the courage to take off the mask and reveal your true feelings, so you can get more out of life.

48. Avoid Alcohol

ALCOHOL IS A FORM OF POISON. Besides poisoning your body, it can poison your relationships, including your relationship with your child. Alcohol is dangerous because it can lower your inhibitions. Any loss of inhibitions means loss of control. You can hurt yourself; you can hurt your child. You never know.

Alcohol can affect your judgment, your ability to think, and also your ability to feel. I once had a counseling client, a teenage girl, who had suffered a terrible childhood. I knew that her mother was addicted to marijuana, so I asked her to tell me a little about her relationship with her mother. The girl calmly replied that talking to her mother was "like talking to a jellyfish." I think the same can be said for parents who abuse alcohol.

You must be a responsible adult for your child, present for him or her both physically and emotionally. Remember that alcohol is not only something you give yourself, but also something you give your entire family. If you think you are dependent on drugs or alcohol and want help, see your doctor or contact the National Council on Alcoholism and Drug Dependence at 1-800-NCA-CALL.

49. Individual Therapy for You

PSYCHOTHERAPY (ALSO CALLED PSYCHOLOGICAL COUNSELING) is for everyone. Whether you are a man or a woman, I believe that you can benefit from therapy at some point in your life. Depending on how you feel about yourself and where you are in your life, therapy may or may not be appropriate for you. In any case, I thought I would take this opportunity to tell you a little about therapy, what it is, and how it works. This way, if you ever feel really scared, angry, lonely, hurt, confused, anxious, frustrated, or depressed, you will know someone to call for help and support.

Psychotherapists are mental-health professionals who help people solve their emotional difficulties. They include clinical social workers, psychologists, and marriage, family, and child counselors. They use a variety of approaches and techniques to meet the needs of each person. For example, some psychotherapists concentrate on your childhood; others concentrate on your present thoughts and behaviors. Some therapists will work with you for a short time; others prefer long-term therapy. I recommend that you "shop around" until you find a therapist with whom you feel comfortable.

Individual therapy offers many advantages. First, the relationship between the therapist and the customer-client is confidential. This means that, with the exception of certain dangerous or life-threatening situations, all licensed psychotherapists are required by law to respect a client's right to privacy (they should not release any information about you without your permission). This "rule of confidentiality" allows you the unique opportunity to get help without anyone outside knowing— not even your husband or wife, boyfriend or girlfriend, parents, or children will know you are going to therapy, unless you tell them. The second advantage of therapy is that it is affordable. Many psychothera-pists work in nonprofit organizations based on a sliding-fee scale, which means that the fee is adjusted to your income level. A typical fee scale from a nonprofit organization ranges from $20 to $100 for a fifty-minute session, and in extreme cases, therapists will sometimes reduce the cost of therapy to below the scale minimum.* This could be the best investment you ever make.

The advantage of individual therapy, as opposed to group or family therapy, is that the focus is entirely on you—your feelings, your needs, your goals. A good therapist will help you discover what is keep-ing you from being happy and satisfied. (The Yellow Pages Phone Directory lists psychotherapists under Psychologists or Social Service Organizations.)

* Prices quoted from the YMCA Community Counseling Services, Irvine, Calif. 1995.

50. Join Parents Anonymous

PARENTS ANONYMOUS (P.A.) IS A NONPROFIT nationwide organization led by caring mental-health professionals, administrators, and volunteers. The organization offers free support groups for parents throughout the country, and I want to share with you some information about these groups.

Parents Anonymous support groups are not affiliated with any religious organization, and parents can attend meetings anonymously (first name only) if they choose. The groups provide a safe place for mothers and fathers to share their doubts, frustrations, and concerns. Together they learn more effective and appropriate ways to parent. Members meet in a group once a week, and each group is assigned a facilitator (a facilitator is a professional person from the mental-health field who provides the group with extra information and support). Members are encouraged to stay in touch outside of group meetings and help each other in the event of a parenting crisis.

While Parents Anonymous does not claim to offer parents a magic solution, it does offer the opportunity to learn new skills and develop a strong support system. To find a Parents Anonymous group in your area, call your local Department of Social Services, the United Way, or dial Directory Assistance. You can also write to the National Parents Anonymous office for more information (*see* Suggested Readings and Referral Information, page 101).

A FEW FINAL THOUGHTS

I HOPE THAT YOU HAVE LEARNED MANY THINGS from this book and added some new parenting skills to your "bag of tricks." We live in a rapidly changing society. Children, as well as adults, are constantly faced with new challenges. For this reason, the job of raising children is especially difficult for parents today. To be effective as a parent, you must continue to learn and grow.

It is unfortunate that violence has always existed in the world, and it probably always will. *But violence does not have to exist in your home.* By choosing this book, you have joined millions of other parents in your desire to live in a violence-free home. And, in your own way, you are contributing to a less-violent world. Try to be patient with yourself. As a parent, you face a long and unpaved road. You and your child will pave this road together. It is a wonderful road, as you know, but one that is often unpredictable. Don't be afraid to ask for help along the way.

In closing, I want to share with you a conversation I once had with a good friend. My friend, who has no children, was looking over an unfinished copy of this book. Suddenly she stopped reading. "I wish my mother had done this with me!" she cried out.

She seemed upset and a little angry. She was referring to one of the 50 Ways; I think it was "Choose Your Battles."

"What do you mean?" I asked.

"This would have been really good for me," she said.

She went on to talk about her childhood and some of her painful experiences growing up. She talked about her relationship with her parents and the various problems they had communicating. She seemed determined to be a better parent than her parents had been.

"When I have children, I want to make up for all the things my parents did wrong with me," she declared. "I want to do everything right."

My friend paused and waited for my response. "It sounds like you are putting a lot of pressure on yourself," I said.

"Maybe I am," she whispered.

"Everyone makes mistakes," I reminded her. "Just do the best that you can."

My friend smiled and nodded her head in agreement. And now, as I bid you farewell, I say to you, my friend, just do the best that you can. Angels can do no more.

SUGGESTED READINGS
AND REFERRAL
INFORMATION

If you want to learn more about child behavior and development, read:

1. Ames, L. B., F. L. Ilg, and S. M. Baker. *Your Ten to Fourteen Year Old.* New York: Dell Publishing, 1988.
2. Fontenelle, D. Keys to Parenting Your Teenager. New York: Barron's Educational Series, Inc., 1992.
3. Ilg, F. L., L. B. Ames, and S. M. Baker. *Child Behavior: The Classic Child Care Manual From the Gesell Institute of Human Development.* New York: Harper Collins Publishers, Inc., 1981.

If you want to develop your communication skills, read:

1. Faber, A. and E. Mazlish. *How to Talk So Kids Will Listen and Listen So Kids Will Talk.* New York: Avon Books, 1980.
2. Gray, J. *Men Are from Mars, Women Are from Venus: A Practical Guide for Improving Communication and Getting What You Want in Your Relationships.* New York: Harper Collins Publishers, Inc., 1992.

3. McKay, M., P. D. Rogers, and J. McKay. *When Anger Hurts: Quieting the Storm Within*. California: New Harbinger Publications, Inc., 1989.
4. Tannen, D. *That's Not What I Meant: How Conversational Style Makes or Breaks Relationships*. New York: Ballantine Books, 1986.

If you want to learn more about stress reduction, read:

1. Charlesworth, E. and R. G. Nathan. *Stress Management: A Comprehensive Guide to Wellness*. New York: Ballantine Books, 1982.
2. Davis, M., E. R. Eshelman, and M. McKay. *The Relaxation and Stress Reduction Workbook*. 3rd Edition. California: New Harbinger Publications, 1988.
3. Goliszek, A. *60 Second Stress Management: The Quickest Way to Relax and Ease Anxiety*. New Jersey: New Horizon Press, 1992.

If you grew up in a troubled family, read:

1. Bloomfield, H. and L. Felder. *Making Peace with Your Parents: The Key to Enriching Your Life and All Your Relationships*. New York: Ballantine Books, 1983.
2. Gil, E. *Outgrowing the Pain: A Book for and about Adults Abused as Children*. California: Launch Press, 1983.
3. Whitfield, C. *Healing the Child Within: Discovery and Recovery for Adult Children of Dysfunctional Families*. Florida: Health Communications, Inc., 1987.

For a little bit of everything, read:

Parents' Magazine

Or contact: **Parents Anonymous, Inc.**
National Office
675 West Foothill Boulevard
Suite 220
Claremont, CA 91711
(909) 621-6184

**National Council on Alcoholism and
Drug Dependence, Inc.**
12 West 21st Street
New York, New York 10010
Hopeline: 1-800-NCA-CALL

BIBLIOGRAPHY

Achtemeier, P. J. *Harper's Bible Dictionary.* San Francisco: Harper and Row Publishers, 1985, p. 874.

Atkins, J., and G. Fierro. *Volunteer Services Training Material, Child Protective Services.* Department of Social Services, County of San Diego, California, 1987, pp. 2–14.

Berger, K. S. *The Developing Person through Childhood and Adolescence.* New York: Worth Publishers, Inc., 1980.

Blechman, E. A. *Solving Child Behavior Problems at Home and at School.* Illinois: Research Press, 1985.

Corridan, K., and G. Hoch. "Fun Facts." *Redbook,* Vol. 183, No. 2, 1994, p. 80.

Corsini, R. J., and G. Painter. *The Practical Parent: ABC's of Child Discipline.* New York: Harper and Row Publishers, 1975.

Dreikurs, R., and L. Grey. *Logical Consequences: A New Approach to Discipline.* New York: NAL'Dutton, 1990.

Fortune, M. M. *Keeping the Faith: Questions and Answers for the Abused Woman.* San Francisco: Harper and Row Publishers, 1987, pp. 22–23.

Goliszek, A. G. *Breaking the Stress Habit: A Modern Guide to One-Minute Stress Management.* North Carolina: Carolina Press, 1987.

Israeloff, R. "Smart Ways to Use Rewards (Not Bribes!)." *Parents' Magazine,* Vol. 67, April 1992, p. 109.

Kiley, D. *Nobody Said It Would Be Easy: Raising Responsible Kids and Keeping Them Out of Trouble.* New York: Harper and Row, 1978.

Lickona, T. *Raising Good Children: Helping Your Child through the Stages of Moral Development.* New York: Bantam Books, Inc., 1983.

Martin, G., and J. Pear. *Behavior Modification: What It Is and How to Do It.* 3rd Edition. New Jersey: Prentice Hall, 1988.

Maurer, A. *Corporal Punishment Handbook.* Berkeley, California: End Violence Against the Next Generation, Inc., 1977, p. 1.

McConnell, J. V. *Understanding Human Behavior: An Introduction to Psychology.* 2nd Edition. New York: Holt, Rinehart, and Winston, Inc., 1974, p. 90.

McCormick, K. F. "Attitudes of Primary Care Physicians Toward Corporal Punishment." *Journal of the American Medical Association,* Vol. 267, 1992, p. 3161.

McKay, M., P. D. Rogers, and J. McKay. *When Anger Hurts: Quieting the Storm Within.* California: New Harbinger Publications, Inc., 1989.

Morton, A. *Diana: Her True Story.* New York: Simon & Schuster, Inc., 1992, p. 213.

Mussen, P., J. J. Conger, and J. Kagan. *Child Development and Personality.* 5th Edition. New York: Harper and Row Publishers, 1979.

Nichols, M. P. *Family Therapy, Concepts and Methods.* New York: Gardner Press, Inc., 1984.

Parents Anonymous. *Losing Your Kool with Your Kids?* (A public service information leaflet.) National Office, Los Angeles, California.

Samalin, N., and P. McCormick. "Lighten Up." *Parents' Magazine,* Vol. 68, No. 9, 1993, p. 173-176.

Satir, V., and M. Baldwin. *Satir Step by Step: A Guide to Creating Change in Families.* California: Science and Behavior Books, Inc., 1983, pp. 180–183.

Stewart, M. A., and S. W. Olds. *Raising a Hyperactive Child*. New York: Harper and Row Publishers, 1973.

Taylor, L., and A. Maurer. *Think Twice: The Medical Effects of Physical Punishment*. Berkeley, California: Generation Books, 1985.

Whitfield, C. L. *Healing the Child Within: Discovery and Recovery for Adult Children of Dysfunctional Families*. Florida: Health Communications, Inc., 1987.

Woods, M. D., and D. Martin. "The Work of Virginia Satir: Understanding Her Theory and Technique." *The American Journal of Family Therapy*, Vol. 12, No. 4, New York: Brunner/Mazel, Inc., 1984, p. 6.

How to Read Your Child Like a Book

by Lynn Weiss, Ph.D.

This is the first book that helps parents interpret their child's behavior by teaching parents what their child is thinking. Dr. Lynn Weiss, a nationally recognized expert on child development, explains 50 different behaviors of young children from birth to age 6. You will gain new insight and understanding into such behaviors as boundary testing, irritability, selfishness, and temper tantrums.

Order #1145 $8.00

Child Care A to Z

by Dr. Richard C. Woolfson

This easy-to-understand reference contains up-to-date information on 170 topics that every parent needs to know. It is organized alphabetically to help parents find answers to questions about their child's development. Dr. Woolfson is known as the Dr. Spock of the United Kingdom, and his child-care experience is now available to American parents.

Order #1010 $11.00

Sweet Dreams

by Bruce Lansky
Illustrated by Vicki Wehrman

Bedtime for young children will always be quality time with the help of these soothing lullabies, poems, and songs. New lyrics have been set to familiar melodies, such as "Brahm's Lullaby," "Hush Little Baby," and "Skidamarink." Lavish four-color illustrations surrounding each rhyme transport children into a rich, nighttime fantasy world that will capture their imaginations and plant sweet dreams in their minds. (Ages 1-5)

Order #2210 $15.00   hardcover

Order Form

Qty.	Title	Author	Order No.	Unit Cost (U.S. $)	Total
	35,000+ Baby Names	Lansky, B.	1225	$5.95	
	Baby & Child Emergency First Aid	Einzig, M.	1381	$8.00	
	Baby & Child Medical Care	Hart, T.	1159	$9.00	
	Baby Name Personality Survey	Lansky/Sinrod	1270	$8.00	
	Best Baby Name Book	Lansky, B.	1029	$5.00	
	Best Baby Shower Book	Cooke, C.	1239	$7.00	
	Child Care A to Z	Woolfson, R.	1010	$11.00	
	Dads Say the Dumbest Things!	Lansky, B.	4220	$6.00	
	David, We're Pregnant!	Johnston, L.	1049	$6.00	
	Discipline without Shouting or Spanking	Wyckoff/Unell	1079	$6.00	
	Eating Expectantly	Swinney, B.	1135	$12.00	
	Familiarity Breeds Children	Lansky, B.	4015	$7.00	
	Feed Me! I'm Yours	Lansky, V.	1109	$9.00	
	First-Year Baby Care	Kelly, P.	1119	$9.00	
	Free Stuff For Kids	Free Stuff Editors	2190	$5.00	
	Gentle Discipline	Lighter, D.	1085	$6.00	
	Getting Organized For Your New Baby	Bard, M.	1229	$9.00	
	Grandma Knows Best	McBride, M.	4009	$7.00	
	How to Read Your Child Like a Book	Weiss, L.	1145	$8.00	
	Joy of Parenthood	Blaustone, J.	3500	$7.00	
	Kids' Holiday Fun	Warner, P.	6000	$12.00	
	Maternal Journal	Bennett, M.	3171	$10.00	
	Moms Say the Funniest Things!	Lansky, B.	4280	$6.00	
	New Adventures of Mother Goose	Lansky, B.	2420	$15.00	
	Pregnancy, Childbirth, & Newborn	Simkin/Whalley/Keppler	1169	$12.00	
	Sweet Dreams	Lansky, B.	2210	$15.00	
	Very Best Baby Name Book	Lansky, B.	1030	$8.00	
				Subtotal	
				Shipping and Handling	
			MN residents add 6.5% sales tax		
				Total	

YES! Please send me the books indicated above. Add $2.00 shipping and handling for the first book and 50¢ for each additional book. Add $2.50 to total for books shipped to Canada. Overseas postage will be billed. Allow up to four weeks for delivery. Send check or money order payable to Meadowbrook Press. No cash or C.O.D.'s please. Prices subject to change without notice. **Quantity discounts available upon request.**

Send book(s) to:

Name _____

Address _____

City _____ State _____ Zip _____

Telephone (___) _____

Purchase order number (if necessary) _____

Payment via:

☐ Check or money order payable to Meadowbrook Press (No cash or C.O.D.'s please.)

    Amount enclosed $ _____

☐ Visa (for orders over $10.00 only)   ☐ MasterCard (for orders over $10.00 only)

Account # _____

Signature _____ Exp. Date _____

A *FREE* Meadowbrook catalog is available upon request.

You can also phone us for orders of $10.00 or more at 1-800-338-2232.

Mail to: Meadowbrook Press
5451 Smetana Drive, Minnetonka, MN 55343

Phone (612) 930-1100   Toll-Free 1-800-338-2232   Fax (612) 930-1940